THE VOICE OF A
QUEEN

Unleashing The Power Of Purposeful Words

By Chantal Santiago

Foreword by Hope Carpenter

Copyright © Chantal Santiago

The Voice Of A Queen: Unleashing The Power Of Purposeful Words.

Foreword by Hope Carpenter

Cover Creation: Alexandra Pinson

Editing: Christian Santiago - Born To Rule Global,
Jasma Sparks - Scribe Empire LLC.

ISBN-13: 978-1-7334030-6-1

Scripture taken from the New King James Version®. Copyright © 1982 by Thomas Nelson. Used by permission. All rights reserved.

Scripture quotations are from the ESV® Bible (The Holy Bible, English Standard Version®), copyright © 2001 by Crossway Bibles, a publishing ministry of Good News Publishers. Used by permission. All rights reserved.

All rights reserved. No portion of this book may be reproduced in any form without permission from the author, except as permitted by U.S. copyright law. For permissions contact via email: chantal@borntorule.global

The scanning, uploading, and distribution of this book via the Internet or via any other means without the permission of the author is illegal and punishable by law. Please purchase electronic editions and do not participate in or encourage electronic piracy of copyrightable materials. Your support of the author's right is appreciated.

♛ Dedication ♛

To my love, Christian Santiago

The king of our household, my covering, my greatest encourager. From the very beginning, you saw this book within me before I even put the first word on paper. You have always spoken to the queen in me, reminding me of my authority, voice, and divine assignment.

You gave me the space to truly operate in the grace God gave me. Before I ever began writing, you supported me as I stepped into being the Queen God called me to be. You reminded me that the *doing* comes out of the abundance of first *being*—a queen under the King of kings, a wife, and a mama. You showed me that before my words could shape the world, they first had to be rooted in the identity God had already given me.

You helped me edit this book. You helped me publish this book. You stood beside me in every part of this journey, lending your wisdom, revelations, insight, and unwavering belief in what God was doing in me and through me. You were, are, and continue to be the best thing that has happened to me outside of Jesus, and you're constantly calling out the greatness inside of everyone around you—including me.

This book is as much yours as it is mine.

I honor you, respect you, love you, and thank God for the man you are.

Always & Forever,
Chantal

Foreword

Words. They're all around us. We're bombarded by them on television screens, libraries, social media, radio. Words in our ears by our friends and family members! Words everywhere. Words are designed to sway us, encourage us, influence us, get us in line, push us to achieve, hurt us, motivate us. Words affect us positively or negatively.

The Bible says that "the power of death and life are in the tongue and those that love it shall eat the fruit there of" (Proverbs 18:21). What does that even mean? Literally, it means that what you say will produce; positively or negatively in your life.

I'm so proud of Chantal Santiago. She has written a beautiful guide to remind us as Kingdom citizens to use our words to say what the King says over our lives, so that our lives will lineup with Kingdom principles. This book will be a game changer if you struggle with negativity and not knowing your rights as The King's kid. May your life forever be changed after reading and applying the principles of *The Voice of a Queen*.

Pastor Hope Carpenter
Co-Founder, Redemption
Author, Speaker, Mentor

P

♛ CONTENTS ♛

Introduction:	The Power Of A Queen's Words	1
Chapter 1:	You Can't Be Regular When You're Royalty	11
Chapter 2:	Speak What You Want, Not What You See	27
Chapter 3:	Your Breakthrough Requires Two Mouths	39
Chapter 4:	Faith Talk	59
Chapter 5:	Speak To The Root	69
Chapter 6:	The Power Of Royal Restraint	81
Chapter 7:	Name Your World, Move Nations	97
Chapter 8:	Your Defining Moment - The Choice Is Yours	115
The Final Mandate		127
Acknowledgements		131
About The Author		133

👑 Introduction 👑
The Power Of A Queen's Words

"Why do you do that? Why do you put limitations on your son? I never have!"

These words pierced my soul with an undeniable truth, even as the worship music blared from the car speakers. My two little ones, Zion and Zara, sat in the back seat, blissfully unaware of the deep conversation taking place in my heart. We had just come from Zion's first dentist appointment, a milestone that I had been both anticipating and dreading. Zion, my almost three-year-old son, is an extraordinary child, full of joy and curiosity. He has the ability to light up a room when he walks in and change everyone's day for the better with his smile. Yet, his journey has been different. Only recently has he begun to speak, and eating? Well, that is something I have faith for every single day.

As we drove to the dentist that morning, I was filled with a mix of anticipation and apprehension. I had rallied all the prayer support I could, and the worship music filling the space around us created a cocoon of peace and faith. I knew this was just another step in a long journey, between the pediatricians, assessments and the pressure to fit into predefined molds threatening to drown out the voice of truth I held onto. Zion was seeing all the specialists, having had all the labels thrown his way. Each label felt like a dagger, a threat to the promise I knew God had for him. But as his mother, I'm his advocate, ready to defend him at all costs. Like a lioness, I would roar against any threat that sought to diminish his worth.

At the dentist's office, Zion was a small but mighty warrior. Despite his apprehension, he walked into the room confidently, his wise eyes taking in every detail. Despite the strangeness of the place, he started playing with the dentist and her assistant, his bright smile lighting up the room. But then came the moment of truth, the examination. Without thinking, my fears spilled out as I said, "I'd be surprised if he even let you near his mouth!"

And then it happened. The tears, the screams. Zion's distress tore at my heart, but he held on. He let the dentist do her job, trusting in the comfort of Mama holding him tightly and the songs we all sang together. Finally, it was over. It ended as quickly as it began. Zion clutched a toy duck to his chest, his new friend, his comfort. He quickly went back to his cheerful self, showing off his new friend to everyone in sight.

Once back in the car, I turned the worship music on again and took a deep breath, trying to calm my racing heart. In the space between the music and my thoughts, that's when I heard it - a whisper so clear it was almost audible: "Why do you do that? Why do you put limitations on your son? I never have."

The truth of those words hit me like a tidal wave. Tears filled my eyes as I realized how often my own words had limited my son, and in doing so, had limited God's promise over his life. I had allowed the natural to cloud the supernatural. Here I was, a queen under the authority of the King of kings, speaking words of doubt and fear instead of faith and power. With a heart full of repentance, in that moment I vowed to change. I asked God to forgive me for every limitation I had spoken over Zion and to guide my words from that day forward. I would declare the greatness I saw in him, not the limitations of the world.

The Radical Change

That day marked a shift. I began to understand the weight and power of my words, not just for Zion, but for every area of my life. If you understand how to use your words, you can live the life you say. As Proverbs 18:21 reminds us, "Death and life are in the power of the tongue, and those who love it will eat its fruit." As a queen under the King of kings, my words carry the authority of the One I serve. When I speak life, things live. When I speak death, things die. The words that come out of your mouth matter. The power is in the words, and the responsibility is mine.

When I finally took a moment to take responsibility for my life, I realized I had become an expert at speaking limitations over myself. When people would ask me what I do, I'd say, "I'm just a mother." While that phrase isn't necessarily limiting on the surface, when I investigated deeper into what I was truly saying, I realized the one word that would make that phrase an expression of my limitation rather than a fulfillment of my purpose - and that word was "just". Here's the reality: if there's one thing I've learned about the power of words, it's that every word matters even if it's "just a mother."

How much of a profound effect did that have on me? It caused me to justify staying in that space by telling myself not to complain about anything, creating an excuse within myself by consistently saying I cannot be more than what I am now because "my precious children needed me". While that may be true, what I didn't realize was occurring was that I was speaking death over my future potential instead of speaking life to it.

God used this revelation to shock my system and get me realigned with how He views things. He helped me see that while it's important to look back and see how far we've come, we must not get stuck there because our past can rob us of our future if we stay there. Being a true Kingdom mother means living in the present while also partnering with the Holy Spirit to shape the future.

I'll never forget that truth coming to light when my spiritual mother told me, "You are an incredible mother to those children. Now get yourself out there. Don't always hide behind the label of just being a mother." Along with what happened at the dentist with Zion, this was the moment I understood that my voice—my words—mattered. The Lord made it clear that there was no more room for fear of being misunderstood. If I were truly operating as my future self, would that Chantal care more about being misunderstood over fulfilling her purpose? Absolutely not. So I embraced my calling and boldly stepped up to co-labor with God.

Everything shifted with great speed and momentum from that point on. Over the span of 9 months, God used me in ways I could not have imagined. I partnered with my husband, Christian, to create lasting organizational health for churches. We would go in as a team to help restructure seven or eight-figure organizations and install a Kingdom high performance culture.

After a few months of partnering together, my husband approached me to ask if I would be the CEO of Born To Rule Global - which is the vision God gave him of helping Christians across the globe discover their rulership identity in Christ so they can rule every area of their lives. At first, I hesitated and stepped back, nervous because I knew what his request meant and the level of responsibility it possessed. But after a few days, the Lord spoke clearly to me showing me that I was ready to lead at a high level so I said 'yes'.

Since then, I stepped into the speaker and preacher God always knew I was, simultaneously fully embracing my identity as an author. I've even used my words to speak life over my husband, who already built a seven-figure business and in the three months I was writing this book, he nearly tripled the company's monthly revenue. My previous fight with false humility was so heavy that the old Chantal would have felt out of place sharing everything with you because I was worried you would read this from a place of insecure comparison rather than Holy Spirit inspiration. But that worry is gone because before I could even put pen to paper, God began the process of transforming me into who I desire you to become after reading this book - a queen under the King of Kings who lives out her royal identity from the place of authority.

Our words are not just casual expressions; they are declarations of a royal decree. As queens, we are called to speak with the authority given to us by God. Our words have the power to shape realities, to build kingdoms, to bring healing, or to cause destruction. They can uplift and inspire, or they can tear down and destroy.

As Psalm 141:3 so beautifully puts it, "Set a guard, O Lord, over my mouth; keep watch over the door of my lips." This scripture reminds us of the importance of guarding our words, of speaking with wisdom, discernment, and the authority bestowed upon us by our King. It also highlights the need for God's assistance in ensuring that our words align with truth and love. This was also the exact scripture that a very dear friend and one of my prayer warriors spoke over me that day on the way home from the dentist.

In a world where so many women struggle to see their worth and struggle with their voices - especially speaking with the authority they have - I see two extremes. Some speak hastily, driven by emotion, letting their words fly out without weighing their impact. Others hold back, remaining silent, fearful of how their words will be received. Also worried about being misunderstood or judged. But as queens, we are called to a much higher standard. We can speak with wisdom and authority, being quick to listen and slow to speak, weighing every word, knowing the power it holds.

We must remember that as queens under the King of kings, our words are not just ours—they are His. They carry His authority, His power, His promise. When we speak, we do so not just as ourselves but as representatives of the King. Mark 11:23 says, "Truly, I say to you, whoever says to this mountain, 'Be taken up and thrown into the sea,' and does not doubt in his heart, but believes that what he says will come to pass, it will be done for him." Our words have the power to move mountains, to shift atmospheres, to bring heaven to earth.

My heart for you and my prayer as you read this book is that you would awaken to the queen within you, fully embracing your God-given authority. That means walking boldly in it. May you use your voice and your words powerfully, not to tear down but to build up, not to destroy but to create. May you speak life into your situations, your families, your communities.

As you begin to take back control of your life, may you see the power of the words you speak. May you use them as a force for good. As a queen under the King of kings, may you boldly declare the promises of God, knowing that as you speak, you are shaping your world for the better.

Our Journey Together

I'm honored to embark on this transformative journey with you. Throughout our journey together, I'll share more stories and principles that the Lord showed me to help you shape your world with your words the same way He caused me to do with mine.

In Chapter 1, we delve into recognizing and embracing your royal identity as the queen you truly are—a queen under the King of kings.

Chapter 2 reveals that every word you speak establishes the very laws that shape your life, highlighting the immense power of your spoken words.

In Chapter 3, you'll discover that you have the responsibility to speak God's Word with the authority and power as if God Himself were speaking through you.

Chapter 4 illuminates what speaking in faith truly looks like, empowering you to declare promises with unwavering confidence.

Moving into Chapter 5, you'll learn to address the root causes of situations rather than just the symptoms, enabling lasting transformation.

Chapter 6 uncovers that true wisdom and strength lie in mastering the art of silence and knowing when to hold back—the essence of royal restraint.

In Chapter 7, you'll find that when you align your inner life with God's purpose, your words become powerful tools of grace and transformation.

Finally, Chapter 8 drives home the profound truth that the greatest failure isn't in risking failure by trying, but in remaining silent and doing nothing.

It's time that you start to see the things you have been believing for to come to pass. If you want to see things shift in your life, start by looking at the words you are speaking over yourself and the people and situations around you.

Speak life. Speak truth. Speak with the authority as the queen you are. Your words have power beyond measure - use them to create the life you desire, to become the queen you were created to be. For in your words lies the power to bring forth the Kingdom of God, to bring forth His will on earth as it is in heaven. Speak as a queen under the King of kings and watch as your world transforms.

Now, if you're ready to go on that journey together to become the queen you were destined to become, turn the page and let's begin using our voice to shape our world.

The Voice Of A Queen

👑 You Can't Be Regular When 👑 You're Royalty

> "But you are a chosen generation, *a royal priesthood*, a holy nation, His own special people, that you may proclaim the praises of Him who called you out of darkness into His marvelous light."
> 1 Peter 2:9 NKJV

"Hey babe, what about this pink jacket? Would your future self wear this?"

There I stood with Christian in our walk-in closet, who was sorting through our clothes and passionately throwing them on the ground. You see, I had just set an impossible faith goal with God to impact 500,000 women in the next 3 years, and when you set such a goal, everything must transform. I found myself in that moment living out the saying, "For things to change, things have to change." The people I spent time with had to change; the conversations I engaged in had to change; the words I spoke had to change; my conduct had to change—and so did the clothes I wore.

I truly needed to operate as my future self now, not later if I was going to make any progress toward my impossible faith goal. These were all aspects within my control, and I mention this because when you're pursuing an impossible faith goal, you develop a new level of reliance on God—without Him, it simply won't come to pass. I give my best and God does the rest.

So there I was, having pulled out all the garments that didn't fit the future Chantal. Christian held up that pink jacket and questioned why I had kept it. In that moment, I realized I was trying to justify keeping it, listing all the reasons it could still work. In doing so, I was holding on to my past self. If I was going to operate as the Queen the Lord made me to be, I had to embrace that my past doesn't dictate my future. You look back only to see how far you've come, but you operate from your future self—the one who has already achieved that impossible faith goal with God.

Christian challenged me, and deep down, I knew he was right. He took the jacket off the hanger and tossed it onto the floor with the other discarded clothes. He then did the same with three more items. With each piece of clothing hitting the ground, it felt like the layers of my past self continued to shed until the old Chantal no longer could see a reflection of herself in my closet. That's when 1 Corinthians 5:20 came to mind, "The old has passed away, the new is here." But it doesn't end here.

What happened next was the fun part: replacing those clothes to align with the Chantal that has already impacted those women to step into their crowns. And yet, for someone who loves shopping, there was something I noticed: I felt the weight of every purchase. Walking back to the car with bags full of new clothes, my heart felt renewed and strengthened - like how I was supposed to feel. This entire experience taught me something I'll never forget: you can't be regular when you are royalty.

Embracing Your Crown

There comes a time when every queen realizes her royal identity - an awakening to the truth that she is not ordinary, but extraordinary; that you have been set apart for a divine purpose. This realization is transformative, for it changes everything. Imagine understanding that you are not just an individual, but part of a royal lineage - a heritage that demands a new way of thinking, acting, and living.

This is not a dream; this is the reality for those who belong to the Kingdom of God. As a queen under the King of kings, you possess a unique identity and authority that sets you apart from the rest of the world. Your life is meant to reflect the standards of the Kingdom of God, not conform to the ways of this world (Romans 12:2).

For some, this may be the first time you've felt this awakening, asking yourself, "Am I really a queen?" But deep down, you've always sensed there was more inside you than what you see right now. You've known that God has greater things for your life, that you have more to offer the Kingdom than you currently are. Yes, you are a queen. How do I know this? Because I've been there, too. It's about realizing that we are not daughters working away in the field for our Father but Queens ruling with Jesus in the palace (Revelation 5:20).

Growing up in Australia, I was familiar with the concept of royalty. The British monarchy was and still is an integral part of our culture, symbolizing heritage and continuity. We understood hierarchy and the significance of the royal family. We knew who the Queen was, and the honor that came with being part of a royal lineage. We recognized the protocols and expectations that accompanied it. Similarly, recognizing our place in God's royal family requires us to understand the protocols and standards of His Kingdom.

What brought this home for me occurred in 2005. At the age of 21, I felt an urgent call to organize a mission trip leading a group of 27 people to a place that had profoundly impacted my life: Thailand. This is a country where the concept of royalty is deeply ingrained in its culture and respected by its people. Yet, it is also a place of stark contrasts - where extreme wealth exists just minutes away from severe poverty. Our journey took us to a refugee camp, a place marked by despair and hardship. Our mission was clear: to share a message that could transform lives - that the people we met were part of God's Royal Family.

In Thailand, where the reverence for the monarchy runs deep, this idea resonated profoundly. The people understand what it means to honor a king, to know the protocols, and to respect the dignity of royal lineage. When we shared with them that they were part of a divine royal family, we witnessed their eyes light up with hope. Despite their hardships, they embraced the truth that they, too, were royal and had a place in God's Kingdom. If embracing the identity of royalty can bring hope to refugees, how much more can it bring hope to your situation if you embrace it?

Living According To Kingdom Standards

Our royal identity is not just a title; it's a calling to live by the standards of the Kingdom of God. Romans 8:14-17 tells us, "For those who are led by the Spirit of God are the children of God... if we are children, then we are heirs - heirs of God and co-heirs with Christ."

Being an heir means that we have rights, privileges, and responsibilities. We share in Christ's authority, seated with Him in heavenly places (Ephesians 2:6), a position that grants us power and influence. However, this also means we are held to a higher standard - a standard that reflects God's holiness, righteousness and love. Our actions, words and decisions should reflect the Kingdom of God, not the center of our preferences.

Think of royals like Prince William and Kate Middleton for example. When they are on royal duties, they adhere to certain protocols, such as not holding hands in public. This isn't about personal preference; it's a reflection of their royal status. Their behavior represents the monarchy, and they are aware of the weight their actions carry. In the same way, as members of God's royal family, our actions, words, and decisions should reflect the values of the Kingdom of God.

In 2 Corinthians 5:20, it says, "Now then, we are ambassadors for Christ, as though God were pleading through us: we implore you on Christ's behalf, be reconciled to God." This verse reminds us that as queens, we represent far more than ourselves—we are ambassadors of Christ. To be an ambassador is to act and speak on behalf of someone greater, carrying their authority and message. For us, that means living in a way that reflects Christ's love, truth, and power. Our words, actions, and choices should consistently point others to Him and demonstrate the principles of the Kingdom we are called to embody.

Being an ambassador is not passive; it requires intentionality. A queen doesn't move carelessly—she walks with wisdom, grace, and purpose, aware that her actions ripple far beyond herself. In the same way, as Christ's ambassadors, we are called to speak life, bring hope, and act with kindness, even in moments of challenge or conflict. Whether it's resisting the urge to respond to negativity, showing patience in difficult conversations, or choosing generosity when it's inconvenient, every decision becomes an opportunity to represent the heart of God.

As ambassadors and being part of God's royal family, we must never forget that our lives are on display for the world. How we carry ourselves, handle challenges, and nurture relationships speaks volumes about the Kingdom we represent. Living as both queens and ambassadors means fully embracing this responsibility, allowing our light to shine brightly so that others see Christ through us. Every word we speak and every choice we make is an opportunity to reflect His character and reign as the royalty we are called to be.

Living as royalty means adopting a royal mindset. It's about recognizing that you have been given a throne to sit on, a crown to wear, and a scepter to wield. It's time to acknowledge the throne God has set for you, the crown He has placed on your head, and the scepter in your hand. You are royalty - chosen by God to rule and reign.

This realization goes beyond knowing your identity; it's about understanding your purpose. Matthew 5:14-16 says, "You are the light of the world. A city on a hill cannot be hidden. Nor do they light a lamp and put it under a basket, but on a lampstand, and it gives light to all who are in the house. Let your light so shine before men, that they may see your good works and glorify your Father in heaven." You see, as a queen, you are called to govern your life with wisdom, to make decisions that align with Kingdom values, and to influence the world around you.

The Protocols of Royalty

Being part of God's royal family means adhering to certain protocols. Romans 12:2 tells us "And do not be conformed to this world, but be transformed by the renewing of your mind, that you may prove what is that good and acceptable and perfect will of

God." It's about living according to the standards of the Kingdom, not according to the world's definition of importance. While the world may place value on power, wealth, and status, God's Kingdom values humility, love, and service.

As a queen, you are called to embody these values. You are called to be a servant leader, prioritizing the needs of others and using your influence for their benefit. This doesn't mean neglecting your own needs, but it does mean leading with a heart of service.

Living with Dignity and Grace

As a queen, it is not just your presence that matters; it is also how you carry yourself. Your posture, body language, and appearance should all reflect your royal identity. Stand tall, move with purpose, and carry yourself with grace. Dress elegantly reflecting the dignity of your position, not to attract attention, but to honor the role you have been given. Speak with clarity and confidence, understanding that your words have the power to inspire and influence. Be polite, considerate, and gracious in your interactions, showing respect, kindness, and empathy.

Colossians 3:12 says, "Therefore, as the elect of God, holy and beloved, put on tender mercies, kindness, humility, meekness, longsuffering." This verse reinforces the royal qualities that we should "wear" on a daily basis - kindness, humility, and grace. It calls us to embody these, reflecting the dignity of our royal identity and the heart of the King we represent.

Embracing challenges and pursuing growth is a vital part of living as royalty. Every challenge presents an opportunity to develop further as a queen. It means being willing to learn, adapt, and change. It's about reflecting confidence and composure, even in the face of adversity. As a queen, you are defined not by your circumstances but by your response to them. Face challenges with courage, knowing that you have been given the authority and power to overcome.

Reflecting the Heart of the King

As a member of God's royal family, your life should reflect the heart of the King. You are called to mirror His love, and grace to the world. Philippians 2:5 declares, "Let this mind be in you which was also in Christ Jesus." In this we see that we are to adopt the mindset of Christ, aligning our attitudes and actions with His. It encourages us to reflect His heart in our words, deeds, and leadership.

I recall when I was working in the residential construction industry back in Australia. I had a coworker whose name will be Emma for the sake of this story. From the moment Emma started working with our team, she seemed withdrawn and would rarely engage with others in the office, despite our best efforts to include her. Many colleagues thought she was unfriendly or uninterested and as a result, she was quite often isolated.

One day in particular, I noticed that Emma was looking particularly troubled. I began to feel this pounding on the inside as though a nudge to check in with her. I went over to her with a warm smile and struck up a casual conversation as usual. I would normally ask how she was doing yet not stop to hear the response and I noticed that others wouldn't even stop to acknowledge her. So this time I asked her how she was doing, I decided to stop and genuinely listen to her response.

Emma was initially hesitant, almost surprised that I cared enough to stop and listen. She slowly began opening up about a personal challenge she was facing at home with her partner. Tears filled her eyes as she told me that he had been diagnosed with cancer and was undergoing further tests to find out the severity of it. Softness came across her face. It was almost as if my willingness to stop and listen without judgment provided her with a sense of relief. Once she had finished sharing, I was able to offer her words of encouragement and let her know that I was there to support her in any way I could.

Over the next few weeks, I continued to check in with Emma on the status of her partner. I would invite her to join me and some of the team for lunch or coffee breaks, helping her feel more connected to the team. Not long after, she became more engaged at work and started participating in team meetings more. Other coworkers noticed the positive change and also began to include Emma more often.

Our team atmosphere had become more inclusive and supportive. The day her partner got the results that the cancer was benign, Emma came rushing over to me to share the news. She threw her arms around me, hugging my neck saying, "Thank you. Your friendship meant the world to me."

Your identity as royalty is not just about who you are but about who you represent. It's about living a life that honors the King of kings, using your influence to create positive change, and be a beacon of hope and love. As a queen, you are called to lead by example, inspire others, and bring the values of God's Kingdom to earth.

Practical Steps to Function As A Queen

1. Get Used To Approaching Royalty
2. Elevate To Higher Standards
3. Speak What You Want, Not What You Feel
4. Be Royally Bound To Your Decree
5. Expect Favor To Flow Towards You

1. Get Used To Approaching Royalty: When I was a little girl, I always knew I could go to my Dad no matter what. It didn't matter if he was in the middle of teaching a music lesson, sitting in an important meeting or in my teenage years walking into his office to just cry with him. His door was always open for me. I remember times when I'd quietly peek into his room, and the moment he saw me, his face would light up. Sometimes I'd burst right in, excited to show him a drawing or just needing a hug. He never made me feel like an interruption. I was his girl, and I had full access to him whenever I needed it.

Looking back, I realize that this is exactly how God wants us to approach Him. Just as I boldly went to my Dad without hesitation, we can come before God with the same confidence (Hebrews 4:16). We need to get used to approaching royalty - the King of kings - knowing that His Throne Room is always open to us. Just like my dad's open door, God's presence is available at all times. All we have to do is step in, knowing we're His children which makes us royalty.

2. Elevate To Higher Standards: What are some areas in your own life that you have settled for second best? It is time to stop settling. I'm reminded of a guest speaker we had at one of our events who was talking about elevating your standards. She was sharing about when you know you are called to live a life of abundance, then you should start acting like it now and not wait until it happens. "Stop drinking water out of a cup and start drinking it out of a wine glass." In other words, don't settle for holes in your jeans when God has given you the palace. You are a reflection of our King.

3. Speak What You Want, Not What You Feel: When we were trying to get pregnant with our first born, Zion, we tried for 22 months to get pregnant. Month after month we would take the pregnancy test and month and after month the test results would come back negative. In early 2020, God challenged Christian and I to declare by faith because "this is the year you will receive your promise." Each month we didn't get pregnant would hurt deeper and deeper. But despite the hurt, it didn't stop our confession of faith. We would reset and continue declaring "this is the month we will get pregnant." Then finally on December 31st of 2020 on a 4 hour layover in Miami airport, I took a pregnancy test and found out we were pregnant with Zion.

Instead of dwelling on our feelings, we chose to speak what we wanted, trusting in God's promises and His faithfulness. By aligning our words with His word, we maintain a hopeful perspective rooted in faith. This not only inspires us to take action but also allows God to work through us, bringing about change according to His plans.

4. Be Royally Bound To Your Decree: Every royal leader who is in a position of authority is very careful with their words because once they speak, they are bound by royal decree. In the same way, let your words be weighed carefully to such a degree that when you release them, you truly carry through with the responsibility of fulfilling them.

5. Expect Favor To Flow Towards You: Royalty naturally expects favor to follow them wherever they go, and as daughters of the Most High King, so should we. We are not just ordinary individuals; we are heirs to the Kingdom, and with that identity comes the assurance of God's unending favor. We should confidently anticipate His goodness to follow and flow toward us no matter what room or situation we step into or situation we face.

It's surprising to see that when we expect God's goodness to come toward us, it actually does. It isn't about luck or chance. It's about living in the certainty of His faithfulness and promises. When we genuinely believe in HIs goodness and eagerly anticipate it coming our way, we open the door for His favor to operate abundantly in our lives. So let's walk into every room with our heads held high, anticipating positive outcomes, knowing that as His child, His favor is always with us.

Raising The Standard

Embracing your royal identity is a journey of discovering who you are and the purpose for which you were created. You are a queen under the King of kings, chosen for a divine purpose. Your life is meant to reflect the standards of the Kingdom, to bring glory to the King, and to make a meaningful impact in the world. You are not ordinary; you are extraordinary. You are not common; you are royalty.

As you navigate through life, always remember that your royal identity calls for a higher standard of living and a deeper level of wisdom. You are called to live purposefully, to speak with authority, and to lead with integrity. You are called to be a light in a dark world, to bring hope to those who are hopeless, and to reflect the love and grace of the King.

You are not just anyone - you are royalty. Live in a way that honors your heritage and fulfills your calling. Rise up, step into your role, and be the queen that you are meant to be. Because truly, you can't be regular when you're royalty.

The Voice Of A Queen

♛ Speak What You Want, ♛ Not What You See

"Good morning, my businesswoman."

I looked at Christian strangely as he greeted me this way - it was completely different to how he usually would greet me. Nonetheless, I kept on with my morning routine. At that time I had my own health and wellness business and I had been feeling as though I had hit a block when it came to growing my team. No matter what I tried, it was as though I couldn't get momentum. It was like I was stuck.

Christian continued this process of greeting me this way for weeks. Each day I became more familiar with hearing it. I even began to take that on as my new identity. The way I spoke began to change. The way I acted changed. There was even one night where I got out of bed after midnight and sat at my desk. My mind raced with thoughts and ideas; with possibilities and plans for my business.

Those words, seemingly casual yet full of purpose for my husband, carried the power to shape my thoughts and actions. They planted a seed, from which ideas grew, and with those ideas came actions. With those actions, results came not just in my business but in every area of my life. The very next month I promoted to the second of four levels in my business.

It makes me think of God's words as He created the heavens and the earth - full of purpose. Not mere sounds but catalysts that shaped the universe. He spoke, and it was. From the formation of light to the creation of humankind, every word from God's mouth carried creative power, birthing reality from the void. Similarly, your words are the laws that govern your life.

Speaking like the King means recognizing that your words carry authority—an authority to create, transform, and establish the reality you live in. Just as God's words gave form to the cosmos, your words have the power to shape your reality, dictating the course of your life. This truth calls for a profound sense of responsibility and intentionality, knowing that your words are the building blocks of your future.

Your Words Have Creative Power

One of the most awe-inspiring titles given to God is "King of kings and Lord of lords." This title emphasizes His ultimate authority over all creation and serves as a profound reminder of His unmatched power and sovereignty. Even King Nebuchadnezzar, a ruler with immense earthly power, eventually acknowledged God as the supreme King (Daniel 4:34, 37).

The way a king speaks is marked by authority, precision, and formality, knowing that his words can become law and must be carefully chosen. As heirs to God's Kingdom (Romans 8:17), we must also understand the significance of our words. The truth is, as the queens we are, our greatest strength is found when our speech reflects the character and authority of our King.

How God created everything in the Creation Account reflects this power. In Genesis 1, God said, "Let there be light," and light appeared. In verse 24, He said, "Let the earth produce living creatures," and it was so. God's words were not just directives; they were the very substance of creation. God then created Man with His very words. Genesis 1:26 reminds us that we are made in God's image and likeness. I don't know if that has hit you before, but out of everything God created, mankind is the only thing made in His image and likeness.

Being made in God's image means having the same moral and spiritual nature and characteristics. Made in God's likeness means to function like Him. Dr Myles Munroe says, "If you want to know how you are supposed to function as humankind, you have to study God. It is when a human doesn't function like God, he begins to malfunction and self-destruct."

We possess the same creative power with our words. Your words, much like God's, are spirit in nature and have a long-lasting effect. The power of our words to shape reality became real to me when we started receiving prophetic words that completely shifted how we saw our future.

Creating A New Tomorrow

The power of words to create new realities became even more evident when we received a prophetic word at Bethel Church in Redding, California and again in Brazil. Many times after being at Bethel we would receive prophetic words over us that there was an anointing on our lives for business. At first we thought that the people who were speaking over us had the wrong people and that the words were not for us. But after hearing the same thing over and over, we began to pay more attention. It was also declared that supernatural financial increase would come to us from the East.

At the time we lived on the West Coast, in Southern California and had been in full time vocational ministry from the time we were married, which had been 4 years at the time. We didn't know what this would look like, but we decided to hold onto all of these words, aligning our speech and expectations with what had been spoken over us. We began to declare financial increase over our lives and business.

Our words were not just hopeful statements; they were seeds being sown into the fertile soil of faith. Each declaration was a step toward the future we were creating, a future shaped by the authority of God's promise. Because of the declarations both spoken over us and from our own mouths directly, shortly after, we found ourselves living in Greenville, South Carolina - on the East Coast. Not only were we living on the East Coast, but God was rapidly closing vocational ministry doors and opening business doors for us. He had our complete attention.

If you want your tomorrow to be different, you must create something different today. This begs the question: how do you create something different as a queen under the King of kings? This requires aligning your words with God's truth and speaking what you prefer, not just what you see.

As women who feel emotions deeply, it can be too easy to talk about what you see or feel in the present, but that's not how righteous Queens live. We walk, talk, and act by faith, not by sight (2 Corinthians 5:7). We live by the vision in our spirit, not the sight in our eyes. That's how God operated. He didn't speak what He saw (darkness), He spoke what He wanted (light). Every word that proceeds out of our mouths should reflect the same divine strategy our King took, speaking life into situations that seem dead and declaring hope where there appears to be none.

In our own personal experiences, we have seen firsthand the power of this principle. When words were spoken over our son Zion, suggesting he was behind and might have special needs, we chose to declare otherwise. We spoke life and normalcy over him, refusing to accept a limiting narrative. Not a lot of people understand our level of faith and more often than not, they look at us like we are crazy. But to this very day, Zion is rapidly catching up, demonstrating receptiveness and social engagement far beyond expectations.

Our declarations created an atmosphere of faith, allowing Zion to flourish according to the vision God placed within us as his parents over the limited confines of professional human diagnoses. This is where I learned that people can be very genuine with what they see, but they can still be genuinely wrong.

Jesus says in Mark 11:22-24 that we can speak to the mountains in our lives, commanding them to move, and they will move. He isn't just giving us poetic language to take to our hearts; He's letting us know the authority we possess in our words that can go unused all because we allow the size of our mountain to define the size of our declaration.

Take a moment to reflect. What are mountains in your life that you've held back on declaring the vision of God all because it seems too big or unmovable? If you're having trouble finding what that mountain is, allow the Holy Spirit to bring up the things in your heart that you're currently avoiding.

Queens, let me tell you something: God knows just how powerful your words are - and guess what? So does the enemy. That's exactly why he works overtime trying to get you to speak negatively about yourself, your situation, and even the people in your life. Why? Because he knows that if he can fill your words with doubt, fear, and despair instead of faith, he can throw you off track from the destiny God has for you. Don't fall for his schemes! He's sneaky, and sometimes it happens so subtly that you don't even realize what you're saying until the words are already out of your mouth.

For me, it's usually when I'm tired or stressed—that's when my guard tends to slip. Like those early morning wake-ups when Zara cries, and my first thought is something like, *"Seriously, is this ever going to get easier? Will she ever sleep through the night?"* Wait a second—she's waking up because she's hungry or teething. It's just temporary, but that's how the enemy sneaks in, trying to make me speak frustration over the situation.

Or after a tough day with the kids, where they've been super demanding and I've barely had a moment to breathe. I finally sit down, completely wiped out, and this thought pops into my head: *"Am I even cut out for this? Do I really have what it takes to be a good mom?"* Nope, not today, enemy! God chose me for this. He strengthens me when I'm weak, and His grace is always more than enough for me and my family.

Moses, one of the greatest leaders, missed out on entering the Promised Land because he let frustration guide him. Instead of speaking to the rock as God instructed, he struck it (Numbers 20:2-12). This emotional reaction cost him the chance to see God's promise fulfilled. This story teaches us that there are areas of our lives that we have not seen the promises of God come to fruition because we have tried to control it through our actions rather than shift it through our words. Stop fighting with your hands and start governing with your mouth. The days of changing things through force are over and the days of using your authority through words are here.

It is time we stop underestimating the power of our words. Our words should be measured and deliberate, much like the King who knows His edicts are irreversible. God wanted the Israelites to speak His word, to align their declarations with His, so that they could experience His promises. Our responsibility is to ensure that our words align with God's words, that we are speaking life, hope, and faith into our circumstances. So how do we start aligning our words with God's truth? It begins with practical steps to speak what you want, not just what you see.

Practical Steps To Speak What You Want, Not What You See

1. Visualize and Verbalize: When you sit with God and close your eyes, what future do you see? Begin to speak out *that* future as though it's already happening. You may begin saying, "My business is thriving," or "My family walks in complete peace." Speaking life starts with seeing it in your spirit.

2. Declare God's Promises Boldly: Find scriptures that reflect what you are believing for and declare them as truths over your life. Just as we spoke financial increase and healing into existence, your words can bring God's promises into your reality.

3. Flip The Script: When you find yourself focusing on what's not working, turn it around. Instead of saying, "This is never going to change," say, "God is working this out for my good." Shift your speech to reflect the outcome you want.

4. Thank God Like It's Already Done: Thank God for the things you're believing for, before you see them. Say, "Thank You, Lord, for my healing," or "Thank You for the opportunities coming my way." Gratitude gets your heart and words ready for what's coming.

The Legacy of Your Words As A Queen

Queens, your words are not ordinary—they are royal decrees that shape destinies, shift atmospheres, and build legacies. Each time you speak, you release power, setting into motion events that ripple through your life and far beyond. Whether you realize it or not, your words are writing the story that future generations will live out.

Imagine your words as seeds planted in the soil of time. Every declaration, every promise, every moment of faith sown into the atmosphere takes root. Over time, these seeds grow into trees—some bearing fruit that nourishes, others creating shade that comforts. But beware, for careless words can also plant weeds that entangle, choke, and destroy. This is the responsibility that rests on you as a queen: to plant wisely and tend faithfully.

When you choose to speak life, you are not just changing the present—you are shaping a future that reflects God's goodness. Words spoken in faith and hope create an environment where blessings thrive, where peace reigns, and where love multiplies. On the other hand, words of doubt, fear, or bitterness can set in motion cycles of despair, strife, and confusion. The choice is always yours.

As a queen, your influence goes beyond what you can see. Just as a king's edict impacts an entire kingdom, your words reach into the lives of your children, your family, and even strangers who hear them. What you say today can echo in the hearts of those around you for years to come. Your encouragement can spark dreams, your prayers can change lives, and your faith-filled declarations can alter the course of history.

This is your garden to cultivate. Every word you speak is a reflection of the King's heart—or it isn't. And that distinction matters. Will your words leave a legacy of love, wisdom, and faith? Or will they leave a trail of missed opportunities to uplift and bless?

Queens, you have been entrusted with a gift that carries both privilege and responsibility. Speak as if you understand the weight of your words. Speak as if heaven is listening. Speak as if generations depend on it—because they do.

Your words, sown with intention and watered with faith, will grow into a harvest that honors the King and blesses His Kingdom. And as you step into this royal responsibility, you'll discover that speaking with purpose is not just about creating change—it's about stepping into your God-given authority.

Cementing Your Responsibility

Queens, the authority of your words is no small thing. It is your privilege and your calling to speak as one who rules with the King. This is not a burden—it is your divine invitation to partner with God Himself in shaping the world around you.

When you speak, you are not just filling the air with noise. You are releasing heaven's will, aligning earth with God's truth, and paving the way for His promises to unfold. Your words carry the weight of eternity because they flow from the authority He has placed in you.

So, speak as a queen who knows her worth and her role. Speak with faith, not fear. Speak with confidence, not hesitation. Let your words build bridges, heal wounds, and set captives free. Let them reflect the heart of the King who called you to reign.

This is your royal privilege—to use your words to create a legacy that mirrors the goodness, love, and authority of God. Step boldly into this responsibility, knowing that when you speak in alignment with His will, you are a force for Kingdom transformation.

Now, we've laid the foundation of your royal responsibility to speak with authority. But there's something even greater at work behind your words. You are not just speaking your words—you are speaking from the wellspring of divine power. In the next chapter, we'll dive into the source of this power and discover the transformative impact of God's Spoken Word on your life and your calling. Let's uncover your Divine Mandate and Power.

♛ Your Breakthrough Requires ♛ Two Mouths

"But what does it say? 'The word is near you, in your mouth and in your heart' (that is, the word of faith which we preach)"
Romans 10:8, NKJV

"And take the helmet of salvation, and the sword of the Spirit, which is the word of God." Ephesians 6:17, NKJV

"I need My Queens to get into My Word."

Here I was sitting with God, preparing to release a prophetic declaration over a group of women on New Year's Eve to set them up for their coming year when the Lord spoke that directly into my heart. As I sat with the heart posture of listening, He shared further.

"It is imperative for what I want to do. Hear My Words—you do not have a weapon if you do not have My Word. The reason why my queens aren't seeing or knowing the true Me is because they are only hearing half-truths. Their true power is in knowing My Word for themselves. Even the enemy knows My Word. But if you don't know My Word or use My Word, you will not be able to discern what is Truth—Me—and what is not."

It ended with seeing an image of a sword being handed to

each woman, and in my spirit, I knew the caveat of whether they used the sword was solely dependent on whether they committed to knowing and speaking His Word (Ephesians 6:17). That's when I felt the responsibility of sharing this word with these women who desperately needed clear direction from God for their upcoming year. And it became a marking moment for me to learn this truth: *You don't have a weapon if you don't have the Word.*

Weeks after releasing that word over them, I began to realize there was another layer of truth. One that caused things to change in dramatic ways and see miracles occur when there looked like there was no possible way. And it's all about whose mouth the Word proceeds from. Believe it or not, the enemy doesn't want the Word of God to enter your heart and exit your mouth because he knows that nothing shifts on the earth until two mouths are involved.

Your Dominion As A Queen

When God created Mankind, He held a specific purpose in mind. I first believed that the original purpose for our creation was to be in relationship with Him along with loving and worshipping Him. While that is essential in our walk with Him, it was not the first purpose God mentions in Genesis. In *Born To Rule: Reclaiming Your God-Given Birthright To Rule On Earth,* my husband, Christian highlights that God's first intention was creating us as kings and queens under Him to rule on Earth as He rules in Heaven.

It was not for relationship, worship, or love that He created us but for dominion. That is seen in Genesis 1:26 when God speaks about creating us for the first time: Then God said, "Let Us make man in Our image, according to Our likeness; *let them have dominion* over the fish of the sea, over the birds of the air, and over the cattle, over all the earth and over every creeping thing that creeps on the earth." This is why we fall apart when we feel like we have no power to change any area of our lives.

As royalty under Heaven, it might not be easy to believe that our mouth contains power to shift the world around us but when God had us in mind, He desired for our main function to operate in dominion. One of the phrases my husband showed me is, "let *them* have dominion", which meant that God chose to have us in charge over what occurs here on Earth.

Queens, that means that if you aren't agreeing with God about your situation and speaking it, then it won't change for you. That's why the only true battle you truly experience is Heaven and Hell trying to get you to agree with them. Whatever version of your future you agree with and speak out loud, whether through faith or fear, will manifest itself on Earth. The power is in your tongue and agreeing with His Word.

The Power Of His Word

The Word of God is not just text on a page; it is the very essence of God's voice in written form. Hebrews 4:12 reminds us that the Word of God is "living and powerful," and John 1:1 declares that "In the beginning was the Word, and the Word was with God, and the Word was God." This means that the Word of God is not separate from God Himself—it is His voice recorded, eternal, and alive.

As a queen, your decrees must be in alignment with the voice of the King. This is why knowing the Word of God is essential; if you don't know His Word, you won't recognize His voice and won't be able to exercise the authority you possess in Him. Jesus said in John 10:27, "My sheep hear My voice, and I know them, and they follow Me." How can we follow His lead or decree His will if we don't know His voice? And how can we know His voice without first being intimately familiar with His Word?

Where the enemy thrives is in the space between ignorance and deception in any area of your life. If you lack knowledge of God's Word in your marriage, finances, health, or relationships, you become vulnerable to the enemy's subtle distortions just as Eve was in the garden, unable to take authority over an animal–a snake–that God already gave her dominion over (Genesis 1:26). The toughest times in my life were when I was unaware or forgot what His Word said - causing pain in my life and those around me.

But when you immerse yourself in Scripture, you sharpen your ability to discern His voice amidst the noise of the world. Your royal authority as a daughter of God comes from your alignment with His voice through His Word. When the declarations that come out of your voice end up aligning with His voice, they carry Heaven's authority, and you can speak with confidence, knowing that His power backs your words.

His Word and Your Voice: The Need For Two Mouths

One of the greatest revelations the Holy Spirit gave me about the power of God's Word in our mouths is found in Hebrews 4:12: "For the word of God is living and powerful, and *sharper than any two-edged sword*, piercing even to the division of soul and spirit, and of joints and marrow, and is a discerner of the thoughts and intents of the heart."

As I read this Scripture, the phrase "two-edged sword" caught my attention. Digging deeper in the Greek, I discovered that the word for "two-edged" is *Distomos*, meaning "two-mouthed." How that verse should be read is this: "For the word of God is living and powerful, and sharper than any *two mouths*." Here's what that means. In the beginning, God spoke His Word in creation. He was the first mouth. And when a Bible verse or passage of Scripture arises in your spirit and you speak it, only then does it become a two-mouthed sword: first spoken by God, then by you. This changes things.

This brought a Kingdom principle to life for me: For anything to occur on Earth, two must touch and agree (Matthew 18:19). Because God's Word is settled in Heaven (Psalm 119:89) and we have dominion on Earth, then for the Word of God to manifest, it needs two mouths: God's mouth and your mouth. Queens, your breakthrough has not touched the earth yet because *it has already come out of God's mouth but hasn't come out of yours yet*. It's not that God is holding back your breakthrough, He's just waiting for you to agree with Him through your mouth. Our King is looking for His daughters to agree with what He says about them and their situation.

For a principle to be solidly established in Scripture, it can be found in multiple places. This principle of speaking God's Word can also be seen in 2 Chronicles 20:1-30, where King Jehoshaphat faces a vast army coming against Judah. Instead of panicking, he prays and reminds God of His promises, quoting from the covenant made with Israel and referencing past acts of divine deliverance. Jehoshaphat stands on God's Word, declaring His authority and faithfulness, which leads to God responding by defeating Judah's enemies without them needing to fight.

The same is true for us. We must align our words with God's Word. If your finances are in trouble, speak God's Word to your finances by declaring, "Finances, come into line, because my God shall supply all my needs according to His riches in glory" (Philippians 4:19).

Will I ever get pregnant? Is something wrong with me? Am I even able to have children?

These were the questions I asked over and over during one of the toughest seasons of my life. After nearly a year of trying to conceive, my words were filled with doubt—doubt in what God had said and who He created me to be. It took two years to finally get pregnant, but what changed first was me. For months, I prayed the same desperate prayers, cried endless tears, and spoke words of fear and defeat. I had done all the "right things," but nothing shifted—until one morning with the Lord.

I was crying, pouring out my heart once again, when I felt a quiet but firm thought rise in my spirit: *"What are you saying?"* It stopped me in my tracks. I realized my words had been agreeing with fear instead of God's promises. I opened my Bible to Isaiah 55:11: *"So shall My word be that goes forth from My mouth; it shall not return to Me void, but it shall accomplish what I please, and it shall prosper in the thing for which I sent it."*

With tears streaming down my face, that day I stood up and made a decision. I began to declare out loud: *"God, You said Your Word will not return void. You said you don't lie. When You speak, You deliver. You showed me our children. And so God, I trust You. You don't lie. From this day forth, I decide to speak life into this situation."* The breakthrough didn't come immediately, but something shifted inside me. I stopped speaking to the problem and started taking authority over it with God's Word.

A year later, on December 31, 2020, our miracle arrived. On a layover in Miami, I took a pregnancy test and saw the confirmation. God's promise was fulfilled, and it began when I aligned my words with His Word. Queens, this is the partnership God invites us into: His Word and our voice. His power and our faith. His authority and our agreement. When we speak His Word, we declare, "Lord, I trust You enough to put my voice behind Your promises."

How Speaking The Word Creates Your Breakthrough

My husband, Christian, often receives profound revelations from God's Word, unlike anyone else I know. When he shares them with me, they are so powerful and profound that I often feel as though I'm left picking myself up off the ground afterward. But then I'm faced with a choice. If I'm satisfied with that second-hand revelation, I could simply appreciate the impact of our conversation and let that be enough. Or, I can take what he's shared, dive into the Word myself, and experience first-hand revelation, allowing God to shape my words so the Kingdom can invade my world.

Queen, when you seek your own revelations from God, you too will find that you can have profound revelations from His Word. You will no longer have to settle for drinking at someone else's fountain because The Lord will co-labor with you to create your own. But once it enters your heart, it must exit your mouth because faith is not truly faith if words are not brought forth. Even the Apostle Paul says,

"But what does it say? 'The word is near you, *in your mouth and in your heart*' (that is, the word of faith which we preach):" (Romans 10:7, NKJV)

As I've gone through the journey of speaking His Word and seeing the miracles that have occurred, I've discovered three powerful ways speaking the Word creates the breakthrough you need in any area of your life.

1. You Align With What God Is Already Blessing

In the past, my prayers used to always sound like, "God, please bless me in this area." or "Lord, please bless what I am doing right now." The ultimate question that always came up in my prayers was: *How can I get God to bless what I am doing?* While that's a question that comes from a pure heart and intention to align yourself with God's will, there's a much higher and better question we can ask ourselves, Queen. Remember, we are royalty so we don't look to ask the same questions everyone else is asking.

Knowing this question wasn't enough, I began seeking. That's when the Holy Spirit gave me a different question to ask myself that changed everything for me: *What is God already blessing?* That question gave a clear, simple answer: His Word. Instead of praying for God to bless what I'm doing, all I need to do is declare His Word over my life because He's already going to bless that. This is confirmed in Isaiah 55:10-11:

"For as the rain comes down, and the snow from heaven, and do not return there, but water the earth and make it bring forth and bud that it may give seed to the sower and bread to the eater, so shall My word be that goes forth from My mouth. *It shall not return to Me void, but it shall accomplish what I please, and it shall prosper in the thing for which I sent it.*" (Isaiah 55:10-11, NKJV)

When you declare the Word of God from your mouth, the Lord will seek to bless what was spoken because He will not allow His Word to return to Him without prospering in the purpose for which it was sent. That's why I continually spoke specific verses over Zion's development, Christian's business, our finances, my health, and our continued impact – with supernatural results coming afterwards. It was not because I'm a more powerful, pure, wiser, or anointed Queen than other women. It was because I made the decision to stop praying for God to bless what I'm doing and started declaring what God already wants to bless. You will get much farther with alignment to Him than you ever could with your own effort.

2. The Word Becomes Your Standard

As I continually declared His Word over my life, something powerful occurred. Every situation that would come up, no matter how big or small it may seem, was now being interpreted much differently in my heart. Declaring His Word created many breakthroughs in my life because the more I spoke it, the more it changed my outlook.

The importance of His Word shifted from being a suggestion to being the very standard in every area of my life. That means if my health was not optimal, I would not just accept it as a "normal" thing every woman experiences. I would go to the Word and pick a few verses, then speak to my health with the authority I've been given as a Queen under the King of kings.

Even in heated arguments with Christian – every Queen has at least one of those with their King at some point, I would not normally lash out like I used to. My responses became much more composed as the Queen I was created to be. How I carried myself even evoked greater love and admiration from Christian.

No longer did I just accept things for what they are. If it did not match what God said in His Word, then I would not accept it in my life. The words I spoke over and over shaped the beliefs I held in my heart. That's what will happen for you, Queen. The more you speak it over your life, the more you will respond like God because His Word now lives in you.

3. Your Efforts Will Be Multiplied

There's nothing more hurtful or disempowering than feeling like you're doing something without help. It's not easy when you give so much of yourself to your kids, family, work, church, or friends only to feel like your efforts are wasted or you're on your own.

I remember moments with Christian when Zion was born

where we used to have conversations where it seemed like I was raising our boy alone because he was working so hard on the business. Even though the Lord was increasing us through his efforts, it still was not easy to have those emotions. After a few conversations, we made the necessary shifts in order to intentionally raise our future preacher in the ways of the Kingdom.

Queen, here's the good news: the opposite occurs when you faithfully declare His Word over your life on a daily basis. You don't feel alone because Heaven actually backs up everything you're saying and God sends help to multiply your efforts. That's right – God sends angels to fulfill His Word and are assigned to help you in all you do. Look at what Psalm 103:20 and Hebrews 1:14 says,

"Bless the Lord, you His angels, who excel in strength, *who do His word, heeding the voice of His word.*" (Psalm 103:20, NKJV)

"Are angels not all ministering spirits sent out to *serve for the sake of those who are to inherit salvation*?" (Hebrews 1:14, ESV)

It means you're never alone, no matter what it physically looks like. You have angels working behind the scenes on your behalf because you are royalty, not the army. Queens don't fight their battles – they have others fight for them. Because you have angels on assignment, it's up to you whether they are actively working or currently unemployed.

What if God isn't moving as much as you'd like because you haven't given His workers a word to fulfill? But once you do,

Heaven backs you up completely and amplifies every word you speak, whether you realize it or not.

Practical Ways To Build The Word In You

There is no greater feeling than seeing something you've been declaring for so long finally come to pass. The joy you experience is like the anticipation I felt leading up to my wedding day, where I had all the dreams of what it would be like since I was a little girl. But before I could get to that special day, I had to first build myself up on the inside to be ready to be a strong Kingdom wife to a powerful Kingdom man. The fulfillment of my dream didn't come until I was internally developed.

It is the same with the words you are declaring. Before you can declare the Word with power, you must have the Word built up in you. Where there is no development, there is no power. Here are three practical ways you can build the Word of God in you to become the Queen who moves her mountains with His Word.

1. Be In The Word of God For Yourself

Being in the Word of God for yourself is crucial for several reasons. First, it ensures your faith is rooted in truth, not merely in traditions or teachings handed down from others. By reading and meditating on Scripture personally, you gain a solid foundation of knowledge and wisdom that cannot be easily shaken. Second, personal engagement with the Word empowers you to discern truth from falsehood, enabling you to navigate the complexities of life with a clear, God-centered perspective.

Finally, immersing yourself in the Word nurtures spiritual growth, maturity, and a deeper connection to God, equipping you to fulfill your purpose and calling with confidence and authority. First-hand revelation makes your faith solid, resilient, and intimately connected to the source of all truth.

Could the state of the church today be because we have relied on second-hand revelations rather than seeking our own first-hand revelation? Second-hand revelations might distort the original message and intention of God's Word, leading to a diluted or inaccurate grasp of spiritual truths. This leaves individuals vulnerable to deception, confused, and having a lack of depth in their faith.

In contrast, first-hand revelation from reading the Word of God is transformative and deeply personal. Engaging directly with the Scriptures opens you to the pure, unfiltered truth of God's message. This personal interaction allows the Holy Spirit to speak directly to your heart and mind, providing insights, guidance, and understanding tailored to your unique circumstances and needs. First-hand revelation fosters a deeper relationship with God, allowing you to know Him personally, rather than merely knowing about Him through others' experiences.

2. Allow God To Change How You See Him

One of the main ways to see God accurately is through His

Word. Yet the challenge for many is that we don't read God's Word with the focus of seeing God. We have shifted our primary focus onto ourselves and what is required of us to be "good Christians." Queen, it is time to realign and make God's Word about knowing God.

The King of kings wants you to give yourself permission to get to know and embrace the true and real Jesus. The unfortunate part is that many aren't reading the Word for themselves. They are relying on what others say. They take what they hear as gospel and truth, whether it be from a new believer who doesn't fully know or a pastor preaching a watered-down version of Jesus that lacks the full power available to us today.

Some of you reading this may be at a place in your life where you are content knowing God only as love. Yes, He is love, but He is so much more. He is also a judge, which means we are accountable for the words we speak and the actions we take.

I don't say this to scare you, but to emphasize the necessity of being in the Word of God for yourself. When you immerse yourself in the Word, the Holy Spirit provides you with personal revelations of who God is—this is known as first-hand revelation.

Unfortunately, in today's society, many people heavily, even solely, rely on second-hand revelations. This dependence on others' interpretations and experiences can be unsettling because those insights might be filtered through cultural contexts, misunderstandings, or personal opinions.

People often ask my husband, Christian and me, "What do you think about this?" or "What's your opinion on that?" Our answer almost always is, "What does the Word of God say?" This response is because it is less about what our personal opinion is and more to do with what is truth.

If a member of any royal family were to gallivant around sharing personal opinions rather than reflecting who they represent, the repercussions would be significant and far-reaching. It could lead to a weakened monarchy, a divided public, and a loss of respect and authority. As royalty in God's Kingdom, we too are called to embody the values and principles of the Kingdom of God, ensuring that our words and actions align with the King of kings.

3. Replace Distractions With Meditating

In our digitally connected world, it can be so easy to rely on distractions – scrolling, binge shows, etc. – to give our hearts and minds a break. With all of the demands we have as women, we need a better source for easing our hearts and strengthening our minds. Our families, churches, jobs, and selves deserve better. That's why one of the greatest decisions you could ever make is to replace your distractions with meditating.

I remember how much time I felt I got back after handing all of my social media access and management to an assistant. It freed me up and became a better wife, mom, and daughter of God. One of the things I did before we could afford an assistant is to simply delete the distractions off my phone. Not even having it there and replacing that same scrolling time with meditating on His Word brought a freedom that I forgot I possessed.

Meditating on God's Word, as emphasized in Joshua 1:8, is central to receiving first-hand revelation and renewing our minds. When we consistently dwell on Scripture, much like a cow chews its cud, we allow God's truth to penetrate and transform our thinking. This process goes beyond surface-level understanding; it rewires our thought patterns, shifting them from worldly perspectives to godly ones.

As the Word fills our minds and hearts, it breaks down the influence of culture, confusion, and second-hand interpretations, allowing the Holy Spirit to work in us directly. This renewal of the mind is not a passive process but an intentional pursuit of God's voice through His Word.

The renewing of our minds through meditation directly impacts the words we speak. Scripture tells us that our words flow out of our mouths from the abundance of our hearts (Luke 6:45). As our minds are renewed by first-hand revelation from God, what overflows from us will reflect His truth and wisdom.

When we speak from this place of personal revelation, our words carry divine authority, clarity, and power. We move from simply repeating what we've heard from others to sharing insights that have been personally revealed to us through our own engagement with the Word. This transforms not only our own lives but also the lives of those around us, as our words become a true expression of God's heart and wisdom.

Stop Staying Silent

Let's revisit the sword being handed to you. In the armor of God described in Ephesians 6, the sword—the Word of God—is the only offensive weapon, but it is not meant for the purpose of a fight. Instead, it is given so you can walk boldly in your authority, knowing the difference between truth and falsehood, between what is of God and what is not. The enemy wants to keep you silent because he knows when the Word comes from your mouth, he cannot fight with you.

This reminds me of when Jesus was baptized by John the Baptist and then led by the Spirit into the wilderness to be tempted by the devil, after fasting for 40 days and nights (Matthew 4:1-11). In the wilderness, the devil tempted Jesus three times, and each time, Jesus responded, not with emotions but by saying, "It is written." Every time, the devil's schemes were defeated.

There is great power in declaring His Word. The bonus is we don't need to guess what God's Words are. Jesus didn't guess; He quoted Scripture, breakthrough occurred, and all we have to do is follow His model. Regardless of what is being thrown at you, just make sure you avoid doing this one thing: stay silent. Your voice, Queen, matters more than you know. Let's use it.

Now that we realize that every breakthrough on the Earth that God sends from Heaven requires us to partner with Him, let's elevate what we're declaring by elevating our faith.

The Voice Of A Queen

👑 Faith Talk 👑

"Have faith in God. For assuredly, I say to you, whoever says to this mountain, 'Be removed and cast into the sea,' and does not doubt in his heart, but believes that those things he says will be done, he will have whatever he says,"
Mark 11:22-23 NKJV

Queens, let's talk about faith. Because if we were truly living by faith right now, how many of us would stay where we are? If you knew, beyond a shadow of a doubt, that stepping into a new city, a new business, a new calling was exactly what God wanted for you - would you wait? Or would you dive right in?

My husband, Christian, and I wrestled with this exact question when we lived in Palm Desert, California. We sensed a major shift and believed God was calling us to Greenville, South Carolina. Yet, we hesitated, anxious about the "right time," forgetting that God's will is actually found in His Word. That's when, on one Sabbath, Christian asked me the ultimate faith question - "If we really believed God could shift everything *now*, where would we be living?"

The truth hit me like a bolt of lightning when I finally admitted, "If we really had faith, we'd already be in Greenville." Suddenly, my own words pulled the rug from under me. It became clear that our delay was never about God withholding direction; it was about us withholding our faith.

But let's be real: many of us believe in God, yet we struggle to apply faith in everyday life. We don't have a "God-problem"; we have a "faith-problem." God's power, provision, and promises haven't changed—our ability to activate them has.

And one of the most potent tools we have? Our words. They can move us forward or keep us stuck. When you combine your words with real, active faith, you unleash a creative power that literally shapes your reality. Let's dive in and talk about why your words, *backed by faith*, are game-changers.

The Nature of Faith

Faith isn't just another Bible concept, Queens. It's the only thing Jesus ever measured during His time on earth. He met people who had no faith (Mark 4:40), little faith (Luke 12:28), and great faith (Matthew 8:10). And Hebrews 11:6 says without faith, it's impossible to please God. That's how foundational faith is.

Hebrews 11:1 lays it out: "Now faith is the substance of things hoped for, the evidence of things not seen." That word "substance" - from the Greek *hypostasis* - means confidence, firm trust, or assurance.

Faith is so real it has substance; it's not a wish on a star. Then there's "evidence." Evidence makes something undeniable. When faith pulls promises from the invisible into the visible, we get proof that God's Word is alive and powerful right now.

Remember how God created the world in Genesis 1? He didn't just describe the darkness He saw. He spoke what He wanted: "Let there be light." His words, *full of creative power*, formed reality. As His children, our words carry that same divine spark. But let's go deeper - and more personal.

A Queen's Faith in Action: The Shunammite Woman

Speaking of lesser-known stories, let's talk about one *powerful* woman from the Old Testament: the Shunammite woman in 2 Kings 4. She's not as famous as, say, Sarah or Ruth, but her faith is extraordinary - and often overlooked.

This Shunammite woman was generous: she welcomed the prophet Elisha into her home and made a room for him. Elisha, grateful for her kindness, prophesied she would have a son - even though her situation seemed hopeless. Sure enough, she gave birth to a boy. But one day, her child suddenly died in her arms.

Now, pause and imagine the devastation she felt. Many of us might collapse under that heartbreak. But what did she do? She didn't waste time wailing or cursing God. She *laid the boy on Elisha's bed* and raced to find the prophet. Even when asked about her family, her words were all faith: "It is well." She refused to speak death over her promise. She insisted that Elisha come with her. And guess what? Her son was miraculously brought back to life.

Notice something: she didn't ignore the reality that her child had died. She faced it head-on, but her words remained unwavering. This is the essence of "Faith Talk": *you may see the storm, the heartbreak, or the closed door, but you speak God's truth over it anyway.* You carry a confidence that your promise is still alive.

Principle #1: Faith Ignites the Creative Power of Your Words

If your faith can't move your mouth, Queens, what makes you think it can move your mountain? Faith Talk isn't just a feel-good chanting. It's the fuel that makes your words effective. Just like a queen's decree changes the destiny of a kingdom, your faith-filled words steer the ship of your life.

When Christian and I realized we were stalling in Palm Desert - despite believing Greenville was our next step - we decided to live our faith out loud.

We put all our furniture up for sale after that conversion and sold it all in a matter of days. People came out of nowhere to cover our moving costs, rent, and even my one-way flight while I was six months pregnant. We didn't orchestrate any of that. We simply spoke and acted in faith. Faith lit the fire, and our words framed the outcome.

Principle #2: Align Your Mind and Heart with God's Truth

Faith Talk doesn't just happen with your mouth; it starts in your heart. Proverbs 23:7 says, "As a man thinks in his heart, so is he." Dr. Myles Munroe put it well: *We live our lives based on who we think we are.* If you see yourself as powerless, you'll speak powerlessness, and your actions will follow suit. But when you fill your heart with God's promises - like the Shunammite woman who refused to utter defeat - your words become unstoppable forces of change.

We see the opposite happen with Peter in Matthew 14. He stepped out of the boat with boldness - great faith. But the second he let fear fill his heart, he began sinking. His heart shifted before his circumstances did. If he had clung to faith in his heart, he might have danced on those waves a whole lot longer.

Queens, the question is: what are you allowing to take root in your heart? Fill it with God's truth, and your words will resonate with power. Fill it with fear, and your words will undermine the very miracles God wants to perform in your life.

Principle #3: Faith Talk Transforms Circumstances

Faith Talk isn't denial. It's not saying, "Nothing's wrong." It's looking reality in the eye and declaring, "God's promise is bigger." Joel 3:10 says, "Let the weak say, 'I am strong.'" That's not a suggestion to ignore your weakness; it's a blueprint to transform it. When you speak, "I am strong" or "I am blessed," you start reshaping your situation into alignment with God's truth.

I saw this firsthand when my son, Zion, suddenly stopped eating solids and speaking at six months. From then until he was three, we battled countless doctor's visits, tests, and concerning words from specialists.

But I refused to let that be the final word. I started declaring, "Zion, you *will* eat by the end of September." By that exact deadline, he was taking bites of real food. God's promises, activated by faith, rewrote his story. No, I didn't pretend everything was fine. I simply placed God's truth above the facts - and the facts changed.

Let Your Faith Talk Shape Your Future

Faith Talk is about stepping into the authority God has already given you, then watching as your words, infused with faith, transform your world. It's a daily choice - just like the Shunammite woman choosing to say, "It is well," when nothing looked okay. And it's your birthright as a daughter of the King.

We see this time and again in Scripture. When Jesus told the storm, "Peace, be still," He wasn't throwing out empty words. He was exercising divine authority. As queens in God's kingdom, we speak with that same authority, bringing heaven's reality into our everyday lives.

Practical Steps in Faith Talk

1. Surround Yourself with Faith: You need an environment that feeds your faith, not your doubt. Hang around other "Queens" who are pursuing God's promises with excitement, and learn from their testimonies. Whether it's your church community or an online group, find your faith cheerleaders and let their words boost yours.

2. Royal Roll-Call: Each morning, list out loud every role you play—CEO, mom, friend, mentor, etc. Then, assign a faith declaration to each role. Example: *"As a business owner, God gives me creative solutions that prosper my work."* By "calling roll" on your roles, you're putting faith in action over each area of your life. It also helps you see every hat you wear as a domain where God's authority can flow.

3. Faith Play List: Create a music playlist that instantly shifts your atmosphere into one of faith. Include songs that remind you of God's promises, and press play whenever your thoughts need a boost—on your commute, during breaks, or while making dinner. Music is a powerful tool to break negative thought loops. It primes your mind for faith declarations by creating a worshipful, hopeful environment.

4. Scepter Strategy Session: When you plan your week—business meetings, family events, personal goals—bring a physical object like a pen or small scepter to represent God-given authority. Hold it as you speak blessings and success over each appointment: *"I declare wisdom over Tuesday's business pitch call."* Associating a tangible item with spiritual authority cements the idea that you wield real power in Christ. Each time you see or feel the scepter (or pen), you'll remember that your words shape outcomes.

These steps are simple but powerful tools to help you live out your royal identity. You're declaring with authority and shifting the course of your environment through the power of your words.

So, go ahead, Queen—pick your "Faith Talk" strategy, decree life, and watch as heaven's reality becomes yours!

The Legacy of Your Faith Talk

What you speak today becomes the inheritance your children and loved ones receive tomorrow. When I was pregnant with my son, I declared daily that he would be a powerful force for God, radiating peace and joy.

Then four months ago, I caught him grabbing his electric toothbrush as a microphone and started preaching into a mirror while our Pastor Ron Carpenter was preaching on TV. I was shaping his destiny with my words before he even entered the world. That's the ripple effect of Faith Talk.

Remember, Queens, "Death and life are in the power of the tongue" (Proverbs 18:21). Every declaration either builds or tears down. So speak life. Speak favor. Speak blessings. Speak the promises God has already laid out in His Word, and what how your future bends in response.

Let Faith Talk Lead You Forward

So, here's the question I want to leave you with: What are you speaking over your life today?

Are you agreeing with defeat, or declaring victory? Are you labeling your problems as final, or are you telling them to move in Jesus' name? Like the Shunammite woman who looked heartbreak in the face and said, "It is well," you too can claim God's promises over any dead dream, any silent hope, any lost cause. Faith Talk is the bridge between heaven's possibilities and your earthly reality.

You are God's daughter - royal by His choice. Now speak like it. Shape your world by declaring His truth, and stepping into the destiny He designed for you. *This* is Faith Talk. Let today be the day your faith-filled words start writing a legacy that outlives you.

Your move, Queen: what will you declare?

The Voice Of A Queen

👑 Speak To The Root 👑

Death and life are in the power of the tongue, and those who love it will eat its fruit. Proverbs 18:21 NKJV

Imagine wielding a power so profound it can breathe life or death—that power resides in your words. Under the supreme authority of the King of kings, every word you utter carries divine weight. They are not mere sounds but sacred tools of transformation, a royal decree to infuse life, healing, and change into your world. To truly embrace this entrusted authority, we must realize that lasting transformation comes from addressing the root causes of our challenges, not just their surface symptoms.

Proverbs 18:21 magnifies this truth: "The tongue has the power of life and death." With this profound power comes a sacred responsibility to reach the heart of every matter. Surface-level fixes fade, but when you speak with unwavering authority and faith directly to the core issue, your words ignite a shift that brings real and enduring change. Let your words reflect God's heart and the principles of His Kingdom, ushering in transformation that is deep, lasting, and aligned with His Word.

The Guarded Heart: The Source of Powerful Words

The first principle in walking in this authority is the recognition that our words are the echo of our heart's true condition. Being that words are transformative in nature, they must come from a place of sincerity and integrity - a guarded heart. As

Proverbs 4:23 instructs us, "Above all else, guard your heart, for everything you do flows from it." Your heart is the wellspring from which your words emerge, and if that wellspring is pure, filled with truth, love, and righteousness, your words will naturally be powerful and transformative.

But what does it mean to truly guard our hearts? The heart, in biblical terms, represents the core of our being - our thoughts, desires and emotions. Jeremiah 17:9 reminds us, "The heart is deceitful above all things and desperately sick; who can understand it?" This is why the act of guarding our hearts is so essential. The idea of guarding our heart is not about building walls or isolating oneself from the world, like so often is portrayed especially in the realm of relationships.

It is not simply a matter of protecting our feelings so we don't get hurt, but ensuring that what flows from our innermost being is aligned with God's truth. A queen who understands this does not speak from a place of insecurity, fear or bitterness, for she knows that these emotions can cloud her authority. Instead she filters everything through the lens of God's wisdom and love.

In practice, guarding your heart means intentionally cultivating an environment where your mind and spirit are constantly renewed by God's Word. Romans 12:2 urges us, "Do not be conformed to this world, but be transformed by the renewal of your mind." Regular prayer, meditation on Scripture, and mindful living ensure that your heart remains a source of life, not a reservoir for the world's negativity. When our hearts are aligned with God, our words will naturally reflect His Kingdom.

Consider Luke 6:45, where Jesus says, "The good person out of the good treasure of his heart brings forth good; and an evil man out of the evil treasure of his heart brings forth evil. For out of the abundance of the heart his mouth speaks." This scripture reinforces the truth that your words are a direct reflection of your heart's condition. As queens, we must be vigilant to ensure that the treasure we store in our hearts is pure and filled with the righteousness of God. In this way, our words become instruments of healing and transformation.

During my pregnancy with my daughter, Zara, I made the decision to step away from social media in the lead up and post birth. This decision wasn't about rejecting technology, but about protecting my heart during a crucial time.

Social media, while a great tool for connection, can be a source of comparison, stress, and negativity. I recognized that if I wanted to be fully present in this new season of motherhood, I needed to guard my heart from these external pressures.

By creating space for peace and reflection, I cultivated a heart that was able to focus on what truly mattered—my relationship with God, my family, and my personal well-being. It was a time to nurture my heart allowing only positive influences in. This intentional decision highlighted the importance of guarding my heart, reminding me that to speak life, I first needed to protect the wellspring from which my words flowed.

Just as a gardener chooses carefully what plants to cultivate, we must be equally discerning with what we allow in. Philippians 4:8 provides the perfect guideline: "Whatever things are true, whatever things are noble, whatever things are just, whatever things are pure, whatever things are lovely, whatever things are of good report—if there is any virtue and if there is anything praiseworthy—meditate on these things."

Integrity means being the same person in private and in public - a well-guarded heart ensures this consistency between our words and actions. This unwavering authenticity builds trust and credibility, making our words more impactful and influential. When others see that our words genuinely reflect the good heart within, they are more likely to embrace our message - whether it is correction, encouragement or guidance.

Guarding the heart is not just a personal discipline; it is a moral responsibility. By cultivating a pure and positive heart, we contribute to a more loving and compassionate world. This practice requires ongoing effort and commitment, as the influences we encounter on a daily basis can easily sway us. However, the rewards - both for ourselves and those around us - are immeasurable.

Speaking to the Root, Not the Symptom

In the Kingdom of God, the call to address root issues rather than simply treating symptoms is a foundational principle. This principle also governs our authority as queens. True transformation begins when you speak to the root, not the symptom. Jesus exemplified this principle throughout His ministry. When He cursed the fig tree in Mark 11:12-14, He did not address the visible leaves but the root of its fruitlessness. This act demonstrated a profound truth: lasting change happens when we address the core issue rather than focusing on what is seen on the surface.

One revelation that I recently received when slowing down and reading the Word left me speechless. I was reading the story of Jesus in the boat with the disciples in the middle of the storm in Mark 4:35-41 and I saw something that I have never noticed before.

To be certain I had read it right, I went and read it two or three more times. Then I went and read the account in Luke 8:22-25, and sure enough it was there too. Jesus rebuked the wind *and* the waves changed as a result of the wind changing. The root cause was the wind and Jesus knew that. So He spoke to the root cause, not the symptom, being the rough waves.

In our own lives, the temptation is often to deal with what is immediately visible - stress, conflict, anxiety, fear or depression. But these are often symptoms of deeper spiritual or emotional wounds.

In the middle of a storm, most people would speak to the waves telling them to calm down when in actual fact, we need to be speaking to the wind. Too many of us are speaking to the wrong thing wondering why nothing is changing in our lives. It is because we aren't addressing the root cause.

I recall a time in my own life when the people closest to me noticed that I was acting extremely out of character, and if I'm being honest, I also knew something wasn't right. I was living in Australia and had been in the residential construction industry working in project management for about six years at that time. I was looking after anywhere from 80-130 clients at any given time. I was in a very toxic relationship. I was angry all the time, which if you know me I am not usually an angry person. I was fearful and had extremely unhealthy habits.

For years, I would spend time doing self-care, exercising and going out with friends. I would pray but nothing would happen. The anxiety would still be there. The stress wouldn't leave me alone.

I found myself having anxious thoughts that would overwhelm me and after putting up with it for too long, I bravely asked my Dad for help. I told him, "I think I need help. Do you know any Christian counselors that could help me?" I had realized that I had been playing this game of avoidance. Getting to the root cause was too painful. After applauding me for asking for help, my Dad helped me find someone.

They gave me some tools to use like how to handle stress as well as time management. We identified the triggers - one being my toxic relationship at the time and feeling like I was never heard or taken seriously. I found myself focusing a lot on the past and nothing seemed to be really working. It always felt like a temporary fix but I wanted this completely gone, not just manageable.

At the time, I wasn't as close to God and one day, after having a major anxiety meltdown, the pain got too much and I told my parents that I felt like this was spiritual. So with the help of my parents and the Holy Spirit, the root was revealed - fear of failure and lack of trust in God's provision.

Once I had identified the root cause, I was able to deal with that and only then did the lasting transformation begin. I began to declare scriptures over my life, such as 2 Timothy 1:7: "For God has not given us a spirit of fear, but of power and of love and of a sound mind." By speaking directly to the root of my fears, I allowed God's truth to address the heart of my struggle and over a short period of time, my anxiety lifted. In this process, I knew I couldn't do this without God and so I made the decision to go all in with God and truly let Him be the Lord of my life.

Shortly after this, the toxic relationship ended. It became pretty clear that we were going in two very different directions and the clarity I had on what I would no longer tolerate spoke volumes. Like so many of you reading this, anxiety is a symptom, not the root cause. It's the same with depression. Being courageous enough to find out what the root cause is will change your life.

This reminds me of what Jesus says in John 10:10, "The thief does not come except to steal, and to kill, and to destroy. I have come that they may have life, and that they may have *it* more abundantly." Jesus came so that we would have life and have it more abundantly. That word, abundantly, means over and above, *more than necessary*. That means that "just coping" or "tolerating" things outside of our divine design is not okay. Anxiety and depression are not okay. Am I saying that they are real? Yes, very real. I've lived through it. But they are also not to be tolerated because "just coping" goes against the kind of life that God designed us to live.

Consider Hebrews 4:12, which speaks of the Word of God as sharper than any two-edged sword, "piercing to the division of soul and spirit, of joints and marrow, discerning the thoughts and intentions of the heart." We spoke of this verse before but this verse also represents the power we have when we align our words with God's truth.

Our words, when spoken in faith, cut through the surface-level issues, addressing the spiritual roots that lie beneath. Jesus did this with the woman at the well (John 4:1-26). He didn't just quench her physical thirst - He spoke to the deep spiritual void in her life, bringing her into a place of transformation.

Similarly, in our own lives, addressing core issues often involves recognizing patterns of behavior or thoughts that stem from deeper spiritual or emotional roots. Things like feelings of inadequacy or fear may drive one to seek validation through achievements or relationships that may or may not be good for you, especially if they validate your feelings.

Take my toxic relationship for example. Not the greatest for me, but fed and validated my feelings at the time. Recognizing these root issues enables you to seek healing and identity in God rather than externally.

How Faith Talk Relates To Speaking To The Root

As queens, we don't simply respond to the surface of our circumstances; we speak to the very roots. Faith Talk carries divine authority—an authority that doesn't just describe situations but reshapes them. "For assuredly, I say to you, whoever says to this mountain, 'Be removed and be cast into the sea,' and does not doubt in his heart, but believes that those things he says will be done, he will have whatever he says." Mark 11:23 describes plainly the power we possess, and it goes far beyond mere optimism or wishful thinking. It is a direct alignment with God's will.

When we speak, it's not about addressing the symptoms. Our words, steeped in faith, strike at the core. Jesus didn't just command the fig tree to wither from the outside; He spoke to its root, and the transformation began below the surface before anyone could see it. This is the power we carry as queens—we speak to the unseen, knowing the shift is happening in the depths, whether it's visible yet or not.

Faith talk is not a passive hope; it is an active declaration of God's truth over every area of life—finances, health, relationships, and beyond. Isaiah 55:11 reminds us that God's Word never returns empty. Just as God's words shape reality, so do ours when aligned with His promises.

When we speak in faith, we are commanding the unseen to come into alignment with God's purpose. Even when we don't see immediate results, we know transformation is taking place at the root level, ensuring lasting change.

Your Royal Command

Entrusted by the King of kings with divine authority, we hold the power to speak life into our domains. However, this authority is truly effective only when it is grounded in a heart aligned with God and used to address the root causes of issues.

When you guard your heart and speak to the root of every problem using Faith Talk, you are not just managing crises—you are bringing about deep, lasting transformation. As you walk in this authority, remember these three key truths:

1. Guard your heart: The quality of your words is a direct reflection of the condition of your heart. Cultivate a heart that is filled with truth, love, and righteousness, and your words will build, heal, and transform with the same.

2. Speak to the root, not the symptom: Surface-level solutions are temporary. For lasting change, you must address the core issues. Ask yourself the question: What's the *real* problem and what's *really* going on? With the discernment given by the Holy

Spirit, go deep, speak to the real problem, and watch true transformation unfold.

3. Declare faith-filled words: Your words, filled with faith, carry the power to shift unseen realities. Even if change is not immediately visible, trust that your words are working at the root level, aligning your circumstances with God's divine plan.

The power of your words lies not in their volume, but in their alignment with God's will. True authority in the Kingdom of God is not loud or forceful, but it is undeniable. As you continue on your journey, remember that your words can cut through superficiality, shape the unseen, and ignite profound change. Speak boldly, speak wisely, and always speak with faith, knowing that the change is already unfolding even before you can see it.

You are not just a queen by title. You are a queen by divine design, empowered to speak with the authority of heaven. Every word you declare in alignment with God's will is backed by His power. Just as the King of kings spoke the world into existence, so too do your words, rooted in faith, have the ability to shape your reality. Whether you are speaking over your family, your career, your relationships, or your personal battles, never forget that your voice carries the creative power to bring about the will of God on earth as it is in heaven.

Let your voice echo the heart of God. As a queen under His authority, your words are not idle. They carry the weight of the Kingdom. In every situation, stand firm in the knowledge that you are called, chosen, and empowered to speak life, to heal, to restore, and to transform. Your words, when backed by faith and filled with sincerity, will not return void. They will accomplish everything God has purposed for them.

As a queen, you must trust that your words, spoken with divine authority, are working beyond what you can see. Speak boldly, speak with conviction, and know that every word backed by faith carries the power to shift atmospheres, change lives, and uproot what needs to be transformed. Speak with courage. Speak with wisdom. Speak with love. And above all, speak with the authority of the King of kings who has entrusted you with His power to bring about His Kingdom on earth.

♛ The Power of Royal Restraint ♛

"He who has knowledge spares his words, a man of understanding is of a calm spirit." Proverbs 17:27-28

"I've been having conversations with some people who've been saying things about you, Christian. To be honest, Sandie and Greg organized a call with me. They warned me to stay away from you, and said it wasn't a good idea to continue working with you."

For a moment, I felt my heart stop. Christian and I were having one of our deep, heart-to-heart conversations in the kitchen. He was sharing some of the things on his heart—visions for the future, challenges he was facing, and revelations about the path forward. It was one of those raw moments where everything aligns, and you feel completely connected. I could feel the weight of his words. In the middle of our talk, his phone rang. It was one of his clients.

Christian answered and put the call on speaker as we were together. Almost immediately, the voice on the other end was agitated, filled with a kind of flustered energy that was unusual for this particular client. I could tell something was off. As the conversation unfolded, the client began expressing concerns that, once stripped of their surface-level issues, boiled down to fear—fear of judgment, fear of failure, fear of stepping out in faith. But what came next was the real shock.

As the client continued, he mentioned Sandie and Greg, two people we had once been very close to. That's when he said it. Once I'd heard it, I couldn't unhear it and everything else blurred in that moment. Sandie and Greg? Those two names pierced me in a way I wasn't prepared for. We had been so close to them once — Christian had discipled Sandie personally, pouring his heart and soul into her, teaching her about the Kingdom.

There had been a time when we had done life together, shared meals, prayed, and confided in each other. But over time, there had been too many instances of unnecessary drama, too many misunderstandings. It became clear that God was moving them out of our lives for a reason. We had distanced ourselves, following His lead.

But this... this felt like betrayal on a deeper level. Sandie and Greg weren't just moving away from us - they were actively sabotaging Christian's reputation and our livelihood. They knew this client was still working with Christian, and they deliberately tried to disrupt that relationship.

To say I was livid, was an understatement. Fury bubbled up inside me in a way I hadn't felt in a long time. How dare they? We had given so much of ourselves, and now they had the audacity to attack Christian's character, to interfere with our business, to mess with our family's future.

I wanted to pick up the phone and blast them both, to defend ourselves, to make sure they knew exactly how wrong they were. But in that moment, I heard a still, small voice—the voice of the Holy Spirit, clear and undeniable. "You don't need to defend yourself. Leave them to Me. There is no truth in what they've said. Don't speak."

It stopped me cold. In that instant, the anger drained away, and I felt the weight of those words. "Don't speak." I realized that by defending ourselves, I would only be feeding into the drama, giving their words more power than they deserved.

God was reminding me that we didn't need to fight this battle in our own strength. He had already seen the injustice, and He would handle it. I looked over at Christian, who remained calm, composed, and unmoved by the accusations. He knew, as I did, that we didn't have to prove ourselves. The truth would stand on its own.

In that silence, I felt a deep peace settle over me. It was as if by choosing not to speak, I was stepping into a higher realm of authority—an authority that didn't need to prove itself with words, but one that trusted fully in God's justice. Proverbs 17:27-28 echoed in my heart that day: "He who has knowledge spares his words, a man of understanding is of a calm spirit."

And so, I chose silence. I chose to let God be our defender. As difficult as it was, I realized that sometimes the most powerful thing you can do is to hold your peace and allow God to work in the unseen.

In that moment, I learned that true strength is not found in how quickly we respond to slander or how forcefully we defend ourselves, but in our ability to remain silent when God asks us to. It's in that silence that His voice becomes louder, His justice clearer, and His hand more powerful.

A queen's true power is revealed not in the roar of her commands, but in the quiet strength of her silence. Her mastery lies in the words she doesn't speak—restraint that shapes empires, a force as fierce as any decree. Silence is not weakness, but a strategic weapon wielded with intention, embodying the depth of wisdom, strength, and control.

To rule with wisdom, a queen must understand that her words carry the weight of her crown. Misplaced words can fracture alliances, spark chaos, and ignite unnecessary conflict. But when silence becomes her shield and speech is sharpened with precision, her influence deepens, her reign solidifies, and she demonstrates true mastery—over her kingdom and herself.

The Power of Silence: The Strength to Hold Back

We are often led to believe that more words, more conversations, and more communication are always better. Culture encourages immediate responses, quick judgments, and constant verbal engagement. But as a queen, you must understand that silence is a different kind of power—one that requires a deep well of inner confidence. Silence is not the absence of strength; it is its quietest and most potent form.

Proverbs 17:27-28 reminds us: "He who has knowledge spares his words, and a man of understanding is of a calm spirit. Even a fool is counted wise when he holds his peace; when he shuts his lips, he is considered perceptive." A queen who masters her speech demonstrates wisdom, for she knows the value of silence. In moments of silence, reflection grows, relationships heal, and thoughtful dialogue is born.

The power of royal restraint lies in the realization that not every situation demands a response, and not every word spoken is productive. It is in silence that true wisdom speaks the loudest.

Wisdom & Discernment: The Pillars of Royal Restraint

Silence isn't merely the absence of words—it's the product of a deeper inner strength. To harness that power, a queen relies on two guiding forces: wisdom and discernment. Wisdom is the insight that comes from experience, faith, and reflection. Discernment is the ability to see beneath the surface, to separate the trivial from the essential, and to know which battles truly matter.

When you combine wisdom and discernment with royal restraint, you don't just hold back your words—you hold onto the truth that not every provocation requires a response. Silence becomes strategic, an intentional choice to rise above petty conflict and protect your integrity.

A queen with discernment looks past emotional triggers and petty distractions. She recognizes that in responding to every insult or accusation, she hands her power over to those who seek to unsettle her. By carefully choosing when to speak, she keeps control. She maintains peace in her kingdom, builds trust among her people, and anchors her authority in a calm, unwavering confidence.

Know that you are capable of high-level leadership. I'm with you, believing in your ability to make wise decisions that protect your future. Maybe in the past you spoke too soon or got drawn into arguments. That doesn't mean you're incapable. It simply means you were still growing in wisdom.

You might worry that staying silent makes you look weak. But the real weakness lies in letting situations, others, and the enemy dictate your reactions. Your discernment ensures you speak only when it truly matters. Gossip, pettiness, and drama feed on knee-jerk reactions. They thrive on chaos. By refusing to engage, you starve the enemy of the ability to gain a foothold in your heart and mouth.

In choosing silence, you demonstrate your trust in God's justice. You show that your decisions are guided by bigger principles than momentary emotion. Wisdom and discernment keep you rooted in your calling—allowing you to lead from a place of composure rather than defensiveness. Even in the toughest confrontations, your restraint speaks volumes about who truly holds the crown.

The Fall of Man: A Lesson in the Dangers of Unrestrained Speech

The Bible presents another powerful lesson in the story of the fall of man. In Genesis 3, Eve was approached by the serpent, who sought to deceive her. In that moment, Eve made a choice to engage in conversation with the enemy. Had she exercised restraint - had she remained silent and refused to respond to the serpent - the entire course of human history might have been different. Her choice to respond led to confusion, manipulation, and ultimately, disobedience.

As a queen, you must be keenly aware that not every voice that calls for your attention deserves a response. Silence in the face of manipulation is not cowardice but wisdom. Romans 12:19 instructs us, "Beloved, do not avenge yourselves, but rather give place to wrath; for it is written, 'Vengeance is Mine, I will repay,' says the Lord." Sometimes, the most powerful thing you can do is remain silent and let God handle your adversaries, addressing the injustice.

Had Eve remained silent and accepted that Satan wasn't worth engaging with in the first place, she would have thwarted the enemy's plan. But by engaging, she allowed temptation to take root. Silence, in the face of provocation, is often the most regal response, as it allows you to maintain your composure and stops the enemy from gaining an upper hand in your life.

One of the most important lessons in leadership and in life is that not everything requires a response. As a queen, there will always be triggers—whether from people, circumstances, or even your own emotions—but the wisdom of royal restraint teaches that silence can be a more powerful tool than words. Proverbs 10:19 reminds us that "in the multitude of words sin is not lacking, but he who restrains his lips is wise."

Restraint is a form of power, not weakness. By choosing to remain silent, you demonstrate mastery over your emotions and an understanding that not every battle needs to be fought verbally. Even Jesus remained silent until the perfect time to respond when He was questioned by Pilate in John 19:8-11,

Therefore, when Pilate heard that saying, he was the more afraid, and went again into the Praetorium, and said to Jesus, "Where are You from?" *But Jesus gave him no answer.* Then Pilate said to Him, "Are You not speaking to me? Do You not know that I have power to crucify You, and power to release You?" Jesus answered, *"You could have no power at all against Me unless it had been given you from above.* Therefore the one who delivered Me to you has the greater sin." (John 19:8-11, NKJV)

Choosing silence and selecting the proper time to speak disarms those against you and demonstrates that your authority is rooted in wisdom, not in the felt need to respond to every challenge. This composure leaves others uncertain and forces them to confront their own words, often revealing the emptiness of their claims. Silence also serves as a shield for your integrity.

Furthermore, royal restraint demonstrates discernment. Not all battles are worth fighting, and silence allows you to focus on what truly matters. Ecclesiastes 3:7 reminds us, "There is a time to keep silence, and a time to speak."

Choosing silence gives you the opportunity to observe, reflect, and only engage when your words will have the greatest impact. This type of restraint elevates your influence, allowing you to lead with wisdom, grace, and authority. Through royal restraint, you protect your kingdom, your relationships, and your legacy, ensuring that when you do speak, your words are both purposeful and powerful.

The Timing of Words is Critical

The timing of words is one of the most critical aspects of leadership. The right words spoken at the wrong time can do more harm than good, while silence at the wrong moment can lead to missed opportunities. Timing is everything because it shapes the way your words are received and magnifies their impact. Speaking too soon or out of turn can create unnecessary conflict, damage relationships, or tarnish your reputation. Conversely, knowing when to speak can bring clarity, foster peace, and transform a situation for the better.

Jesus serves as the ultimate example of understanding the timing of words. Throughout His ministry, He displayed impeccable timing in the way He spoke - or chose not to speak. When the Pharisees and Sadducees demanded signs from Him, trying to trap Him, Jesus refused to respond on their terms (Matthew 16:1-4). He refused to perform miracles on demand, knowing that His actions were to be in alignment with God's will and not to satisfy human desires or expectations.

This act of restraint was not weakness but wisdom—Jesus understood the significance of timing, and that to act or speak prematurely would be out of sync with the divine purpose.

As a queen, you must recognize that your words, too, carry weight and must be aligned with wisdom and divine timing. Speaking at the wrong moment, especially out of frustration or emotional impulse, can create lasting consequences. A well-timed word, however, can defuse tension, inspire action, or bring healing.

The key is discernment—learning to listen carefully to both the situation and the voice of God before deciding whether to speak or remain silent. Like Jesus, your power is not only in your ability to speak but in your understanding of when your words will have the most transformative impact.

There are times when it is crucial to remember that sometimes silence can allow situations to unfold and reveal their true nature, offering you a clearer perspective on what needs to be said and when.

Speaking too early can muddy the waters, while waiting for the right moment can give your words a precision that cuts through confusion and brings truth into the light. When a queen chooses to wait and speak only when necessary, her words are received with greater respect and consideration. They carry the potential to shift the atmosphere.

Mastering the timing of words is a reflection of wisdom, patience, and self-control. A queen doesn't speak simply because she has the authority to do so. She speaks because she knows her words, when spoken at the right time, have the power to influence lives, resolve conflict, and inspire action. Whether you are leading a kingdom, a family, or a team, your ability to gauge the right time to speak is essential for ensuring that your words carry the full force of their intended impact.

Being Quick to Listen and Slow to Speak

Being quick to listen and slow to speak is a mark of true leadership. In James 1:19, we are reminded of this key principle in leadership: "Let every man be swift to hear, slow to speak, slow to wrath." Listening is a skill that many overlook, but for a queen, it is a vital tool for understanding the needs, desires, and challenges of those under her care.

A queen who listens intently shows her people that their voices matter, that their concerns are valid, and that their perspectives are worth considering. This simple act of listening creates a bond of trust, laying the foundation for a kingdom built on respect and empathy.

Being slow to speak fosters both humility and patience—two essential qualities for effective leadership. When we speak too quickly, we run the risk of making judgments or decisions based on incomplete information. This haste can lead to misunderstandings, unnecessary conflict, or poor decision-making.

However, when a queen is slow to speak, she demonstrates a commitment to thoughtful decision-making, ensuring that her words are grounded in wisdom. This patience strengthens her authority because it shows she values reflection over impulsive reactions.

Listening also opens the door to greater understanding. In moments of tension or conflict, it's easy to let emotions cloud judgment and rush into speech. However, when you take the time to listen, you give yourself the space to understand the deeper layers of the situation. You can sense not just the words being spoken, but the emotions and motivations behind them. This ability to listen beyond the surface gives you the insight to respond with wisdom rather than reacting to surface-level frustrations. In this way, listening becomes a tool of discernment and empathy.

Silence, too, serves as a tool of reflection. Royal restraint teaches that not every situation demands an immediate response. In fact, in the heat of the moment, emotions can overpower reason, leading to regrettable words.

When emotions are high, wisdom and understanding is low. By pausing to listen and reflect, you give yourself the opportunity to cool your emotions, seek divine guidance, and ensure that when you do speak, your words are constructive, purposeful, and healing. Silence allows you to gather your thoughts, weigh the consequences of your words, and speak with clarity and intention.

Ultimately, being quick to listen and slow to speak positions you as a leader of integrity. It shows that you are not driven by the need to assert your power but by the desire to understand and lead with wisdom. When practiced consistently, this approach fosters harmony, deepens relationships, and cultivates an environment where words are valued and not wasted. As a queen, your ability to listen first and speak wisely strengthens your reign, ensuring that your influence is both impactful and enduring.

Jesus: The Ultimate Example

Jesus stands as the ultimate model of royal restraint, demonstrating through His life and ministry the profound power of silence in the face of provocation. At every moment, He had the authority and ability to respond to His enemies with divine power, signs, and miracles. Yet, time and time again, Jesus chose silence over spectacle, restraint over retaliation.

In Matthew 27:39-44, as He hung on the cross, mocked by those who doubted Him, they taunted Him to come down and prove His divinity. But Jesus did not take the bait. Instead, He remained silent, fully surrendering to God's plan.

This act of restraint is a profound lesson in faith and submission. It takes immeasurable strength to remain silent when unjustly accused, ridiculed, or misunderstood, especially when we possess the power to silence the critics. Yet, Jesus teaches us that true power is not found in defending ourselves against every accusation but in knowing when to speak and when to trust God to handle our defense.

His refusal to respond to those who sought to discredit Him is a powerful testament to His unwavering faith in the Father's plan. It was a declaration that His purpose was greater than the temporary judgments of men.

As queens, we must learn to adopt this kind of royal restraint in our own lives. It takes faith to remain silent when our integrity is questioned or when we face opposition. But in those moments, we must trust that God sees the bigger picture and will handle the situation according to His will. Our silence can often speak louder than words because it shows that our faith is not in human approval but in God's divine plan. Jesus' life is a testimony to the power of silence and trust in the Father's timing.

When we practice royal restraint like Jesus, we demonstrate that our strength comes not from our ability to respond to every challenge but from our reliance on God's wisdom and justice. Jesus' silence on the cross was not a moment of defeat but the ultimate expression of victory. His restraint was rooted in the knowledge that God's plan was far greater than any earthly taunts or insults.

As queens, we must learn to trust in that same divine plan, knowing that sometimes silence is the greatest testimony of our faith. In our own lives, when we adopt this kind of restraint, we mirror Christ's strength, showing that we are not ruled by the demands of others but by the higher calling of obedience to God.

The Majesty of Silence

The power of royal restraint is the mark of a true queen. It is not in how often you speak but in how wisely you choose your words. By embracing silence as a tool of wisdom, you elevate your leadership, foster peace in your relationships, and protect your integrity.

As you walk in your royal calling, remember that silence is not a void—it is a strategic act. It creates space for reflection, for God's wisdom, and for purposeful action. By mastering the power of royal restraint, you wield a tool that has the potential to transform not only your Kingdom but the lives of those who look to you for guidance. In your silence, you speak volumes.

Now that we have embraced this powerful position in the Kingdom of royal restraint, let's step into one of the final steps in our journey – and it's all about how to enhance every word you speak to move your world and nations like Deborah did.

The Voice Of A Queen

♛ Name Your World, Move Nations ♛

"Thank You for our family, God. Thank You for the children that You are entrusting to us. We commit to raising them in Your ways. Thank You for the impact they will have on this earth for You. Thank You for the purpose that You have already placed in them and that they already exist in Your eyes."

This was one of many prayers that Christian and I prayed long before we were pregnant. We had begun seeking God's guidance in choosing our children's names. In the Hebrew culture, names were not chosen lightly - they were viewed as prophetic declarations of a person's identity and destiny. This is also why Christian and I felt such a profound responsibility to select names that would speak to our children's purpose and character.

During this time, God gave me a vision of who our children would become and even what they would look like. This vision wasn't just a fleeting thought but a profound impression that shaped our understanding of their futures. We knew the names we would choose needed to resonate with this vision and serve as a declaration of the destinies God had set before them.

As we sought God, He led us to two names: Zion and Zara. These names not only reflected the vision but also carried deep, powerful meanings that aligned with what God was calling them to be.

Zion, in Hebrew, means "marked" or "distinctive." It also means "raised up" and is closely associated with the city of Jerusalem, the heart of God's people, representing a place of both strength and promise as well as divine presence. By naming our son Zion, we felt we were declaring him to be a man marked for greatness, distinct in his calling and set apart to carry the strength of a lion.

His middle name, Leo, further amplifies this sense of bravery and leadership, symbolizing a fierce protector and one destined to stand boldly in his identity. Together, Zion Leo signifies a future rooted in divine purpose, a place where he will thrive as a leader and a man of strength and courage.

For our daughter, Zara Eden, the meanings we discovered were equally profound. Zara, derived from Hebrew, means "princess" or "radiant." It captures the image of a woman destined for royalty, someone who carries grace, beauty and influence. We believe this name speaks to her role as a leader in her own right, holding the radiance of God's presence.

Her middle name, Eden, refers to "delight" or "paradise" which echoes the perfection of the Garden of Eden. It suggests a life of peace, abundance and beauty - a reflection of God's original intent for humanity. Together, Zara Eden encapsulates a legacy of grace, beauty and the ability to bring forth life and joy wherever she goes.

Your Name: A Promise And A Purpose

Hearing about how these names carry such weight and purpose might make you think about your own name and its meaning. Names are more than labels; they represent identity, destiny, and the specific call God has on your life. In Genesis 12:2, God promises Abram, "I will make your name great," tying the significance of one's name to God's larger plan. Perhaps your name has a deep meaning that resonates with you - or maybe you've discovered something about your name that feels disconnected from who you are.

Remember, God can redefine and repurpose any name or identity to align with His vision and promises. Just as He changed Abram's name to Abraham in Genesis 17:5, marking a shift in destiny and purpose, He can do the same for you. If you discover aspects of your name that don't resonate or carry less-than-ideal connotations, take heart: God sees beyond what's written on a birth certificate. He can transform your name and identity to fulfill His promises in your life. Seek Him, and trust that He will bring meaningful purpose to your name - no matter how it started.

Who was Deborah?

In our journey of seeking God's purpose for our children, I was deeply moved by the story of Deborah. Just as we carefully chose the names Zion and Zara to reflect the destinies we believe God has set before them, Deborah's life exemplifies the profound impact of a name and calling aligned with divine purpose.

Deborah was a multifaceted leader in Israel—a wife, mother, intercessor, prophetess, judge, and national deliverer. Each of these roles showcased her deep connection with God and her significant influence on the people of Israel. The meaning of her name, "Deborah," which translates to "honeybee," adds another layer to her remarkable story.

Psalm 119:103 captures the essence of her name: "How sweet are Your words to my taste, sweeter than honey to my mouth!" Deborah's words, inspired by God, carried the sweetness of divine wisdom and the sting of righteous justice. The honeybee metaphor is deeply significant. Bees produce honey, a symbol of abundance, wisdom, and sustenance. They work diligently, communicate effectively, and protect their hive fiercely. Similarly, Deborah's leadership brought wisdom and healing to those who sought her counsel, while her judgments were decisive and capable of driving out the enemies of God.

The name "Deborah" is also linked to the Hebrew word for "to speak" or "to promise," connecting her directly to the Word of God. Her prophetic utterances were not ordinary; they were transformative, providing nourishment and strength much like honey does. Like Deborah, our daughter Zara is called to be a leader - a liaison - for people to be able to see God's presence manifested. Her words will be powerful yet sweet, bringing people in contact with the King of kings.

God revealed to me a vision of an army of women — queens — whom He is raising up in these times, much like

Deborah. These women will carry words that have the power to sting the enemy while offering sweetness and compassion to those in need. Their voices will be instruments of God's power, capable of encouraging and uplifting themselves and others in the Lord.

You are that woman—a queen.

In this vision, God is calling you to rise up with the same anointing that rested upon Deborah. You are called to be a woman whose words are not only wise but powerful—sweet to those who need healing and truth, yet fierce and unyielding against the forces of darkness. Just as Deborah led Israel with courage and conviction, so too are you called to lead, to speak, and to act with the authority God has given you.

As you embrace your role, remember that the essence of Deborah—the honeybee—lives within you. Your words are not insignificant; they are powerful and needed. Speak with the authority of a queen, knowing your voice carries the weight of divine purpose. Let your words be as sweet as honey, yet potent enough to pierce through darkness, bringing light and life wherever you go.

In stepping into this calling, you join a legacy of powerful women who have used their voices to shape history. Like Deborah, your words can move mountains, inspire nations, and bring about God's will on earth. Align your heart with God's Word, and your speech will become a divine instrument, cutting through the noise of the world and delivering truth with clarity and grace. As Christian and I prayed for our children and named them with purpose, we see that same intentionality in you. Embrace the anointing God has placed on your life.

The Difference Between Honeybees and Wasps

The contrast between honeybees and wasps serves as a profound metaphor for the power of words and the spirit in which they are spoken. Honeybees, though they possess the ability to sting when provoked, are by nature gentle and industrious. Their primary focus is on producing honey—a substance renowned for its sweetness, nourishment, and healing properties. In contrast, wasps are naturally more aggressive and cannot produce honey. Their actions and demeanor are characterized by hostility, and their stings are often unprovoked, causing pain without purpose or benefit.

In the spiritual context, women with a honeybee-like spirit embody qualities of gentleness, productivity, and a focus on contributing to the well-being of others. Their words, like honey, are sweet, healing, and filled with wisdom. They speak with intention, using their voices to uplift, encourage, and bring light to those around them. These women are peacemakers, advisors, and leaders - much like Deborah, whose words carried the weight of divine wisdom and authority. Her speech was not only a tool for communication but a means of delivering God's will, calming the weary, guiding the lost, and inspiring action.

On the other hand, women with a wasp-like spirit exhibit aggression, bitterness, and often a destructive use of their words. Their speech may be laced with seduction or malice, and rather than building up, it tears down.

The ancient rabbis referred to this destructive use of speech as the "third tongue," a term that encapsulates the damaging effect of slander, gossip, and evil speaking. This "third tongue" destroys not only the person being spoken about but also the speaker themselves. It reflects a spirit that is not aligned with the fruit of the Spirit, which includes love, kindness, and self-control.

Scripture underscores the importance of the words we choose to speak. In Matthew 15:11, Jesus teaches, "Not what goes into the mouth defiles a man; but what comes out of the mouth, this defiles a man." This profound statement highlights that it is not external factors that corrupt us, but rather the words we speak, which flow from the condition of our hearts. Words can lead to defilement and destruction if not carefully chosen and spoken with the right spirit.

Deborah's life exemplifies the power of words used rightly. As a judge and prophetess, she was entrusted with the responsibility of settling disputes and providing counsel to the people of Israel. Her role was not just to speak, but to speak words that were divinely inspired, bringing peace and guidance to those in need. In Judges 4:6-7, Deborah's words to Barak were not mere suggestions; they were prophetic instructions from God. She told Barak to deploy troops at Mount Tabor, assuring him of the Lord's promise of victory. Her words were decisive and filled with faith, inspiring Barak to take action, despite his initial hesitation.

Deborah's influence and leadership were so profound that they mobilized an entire nation to rise up against their oppressors. Her words moved Israel to action, demonstrating the incredible power of speech when it is aligned with God's will. Her speech was not aggressive or destructive like that of a wasp; instead, it was purposeful, healing, and infused with divine wisdom - much like the honey produced by bees.

The Queen Bee and God's Queens

When discussing honeybees, we often focus on their collective nature, but it's also important to consider the crucial role of the Queen bee - especially now that we're talking about queens in a spiritual sense. In a beehive, the queen bee is essential to the hive's survival and growth. She lays the eggs, ensuring the continuation and expansion of the colony. She also emits signals - pheromones - that guide and unify the other bees.

In the same way, God has instilled a unique set of qualities in His queens - His daughters. Like the queen bee, you have the ability to nurture, lead, and ensure the spiritual growth of those around you. Your words and actions, aligned with God's will, can hold a unifying influence, rallying others to move in harmony toward God's plan. This queenly authority isn't about self-elevation; it's about fulfilling your God-given purpose with grace and strength, just as the queen bee faithfully fulfills her role in the hive.

Mastering The Flesh: Overcoming The True Battle For Our Words

God has given women the powerful weapon of words. While the enemy's attacks on our speech are real, our greatest challenge often comes from within—our own flesh. Though the enemy has been defeated through Christ's victory, our flesh remains a daily battle we must face. Mastering our desires, impulses, and tendencies is where true victory lies.

As women, we must be vigilant about the words we speak and the conversations we engage in because our words carry immense power. They can build up or tear down, bless or curse. Scripture reminds us that "out of the abundance of the heart the mouth speaks" (Matthew 12:34 NKJV). Our speech reflects our inner life, and when it is corrupted, it can distort the unique beauty and strength God has placed within us.

The enemy may set traps, but it is our flesh that falls into them. How often have we spoken words we later regretted or engaged in ungodly conversations? These moments are not just external attacks but instances where our flesh chose to act contrary to the Spirit within us. Maintaining the purity of our hearts and minds is crucial in resisting the temptations of the flesh and aligning our words with God's purpose.

Producing Words As Sweet As Honey

Deborah stands as a powerful example of leadership, wisdom, and the divine authority granted to those who embrace their God-given roles without hesitation. Her story in the Book of Judges is not just a tale of a prophetess and judge; it is a profound lesson in the power of words and the importance of seeing oneself as a significant force in the world. Here are some practical steps to produce words as sweet as honey:

1. Daily Immersion in God's Word: Transforming Your Heart and Influencing Your Speech.

Daily immersing yourself in God's Word is vital for transforming your heart and shaping your speech. The Scriptures are living and powerful, capable of influencing your thoughts and words. Psalm 119:103 beautifully captures this, saying, "How sweet are Your words to my taste, sweeter than honey to my mouth!" This sweetness reflects the profound impact God's Word has when fully embraced.

Ezekiel's story illustrates this truth vividly. Before delivering God's message to rebellious Israel, Ezekiel was commanded to eat a scroll—a symbolic act of deeply internalizing God's Word. He describes it as being "like honey in sweetness" (Ezekiel 3:2-3). Just as Ezekiel had to consume the Word to fulfill his calling, we too must absorb Scripture daily to let it nourish our hearts, shape our actions, and guide our speech.

For women, this process is especially crucial. As Scripture transforms our hearts, our speech reflects its truths, offering words of encouragement, wisdom, and healing. The Word of God, both sweet and powerful, teaches, corrects, and aligns our speech with God's will, ensuring that our words build up rather than tear down.

The transformation from immersing in God's Word benefits not just ourselves but also those around us. As our hearts fill with divine truth, our words naturally reflect it, becoming instruments of healing, restoration, and encouragement. Through this, we extend God's influence, empowering others to live victoriously.

2. Pursue Wisdom With The Mindset of Embracing Prosperity.

Wisdom is more than knowledge—it's the application of your insight that leads to true prosperity for you and those around you. When our hearts align with God's Word, wisdom flows like a refreshing stream, bringing life, healing, and restoration. This wisdom, like honey, is sweet and healing, capable of transforming lives.

In the Bible, honey symbolizes abundance and prosperity, reflecting the nourishing and restorative power of godly wisdom. Proverbs 24:13-14 likens wisdom to honey, encouraging us to embrace it as nourishment for our souls: "My son, eat honey because it is good, and the honeycomb which is sweet to your taste; So shall the knowledge of wisdom be to your soul; If you have found it, there is a prospect, and your hope will not be cut off."

Just as honey provides energy and health, wisdom fuels our spiritual lives, guiding decisions, shaping character, and influencing others. This wisdom is not meant to be kept but shared, multiplying its impact. As we grow in wisdom, our words and actions bring encouragement and healing, leading others toward a life of abundance and peace.

3. Be An Agitator for Change.

Deborah, a judge and prophetess, was a powerful agitator for Israel, stirring discussions about the nation's spiritual decline. Like a bee that disrupts a room, her presence and words provoked necessary conversations and actions. We are called to be similar agitators, challenging the status quo and inspiring transformation.

As queens in our own right, we must engage in uncomfortable conversations, especially when pursuing big goals. Like Deborah, we should not shrink back but embrace our divine purpose, using our influence to shift discussions and focus on needed changes. Your willingness to be an agitator can lead to profound transformation, both for yourself and those around you.

4. Move Nations With Your Words.

We had been in Cusco, Peru for about 10 days at this point as Christian and I were the project directors on a week long mission trip and we had been assigned to look after the Cusco region. Four days prior, over 300 missionaries from all over the United States had arrived in Cusco ready to join us. I found myself sitting in the Director of Education's office with my pastor. She was a very powerful and influential woman and knew the weight of her words on the education sector of Cusco. We sat there listening to her sharing her heart and that's when the Lord had me give her a word of encouragement.

God used me to speak to her spirit woman and remind her of the power of her voice and how she is needed. It was almost as if, with those very words being spoken, she sat up straighter and smiled at me. I was able to share with her that her role in the education of the children in Cusco was a part of God's plan for Cusco.

Deborah's story highlights the immense power of recognizing and embracing your role in God's plan. She didn't wait for others to lead; she took the mantle herself, using her words to inspire and galvanize an entire nation. Her speech was a catalyst for change, igniting courage in Barak and leading ten thousand men into battle.

Like Deborah, the Director of Education knew the fight against the education system was spiritual and she knew her role was important as the advocate for the children of Cusco. She led the charge of protecting their rights and had their best interest at heart. She was equipped by God and clear on her strategy. She was able to turn district after district and had great influence in the communities.

Judges 4:9 illustrates this power: "Then Deborah arose and went with Barak to Kedesh." This is more than history—it's a testament to how one person, fully aware of their importance and equipped with the right words, can move nations. Deborah's example teaches us that true leaders see themselves as essential instruments of God's purpose, using their words to inspire, lead, and enact change.

Embrace Your Importance

I have been blessed with many opportunities to speak, share and preach over the years. In the lead-up and preparation of each moment, I would close my eyes and visualize the impact that God would have in those moments and I would see the powerful encounters. I would see my roar. Yet each time I would get up there, something else would happen. Rather than my roar coming out, it was anything but a roar. It would still move some people, but not to the full extent that I had seen while visualizing with God. I would always leave those opportunities feeling disappointed.

Then Christian and I got the opportunity to go to Brazil with an organization that is very near and dear to our hearts, Dunamis Greenhouse. It is a revival school like no other. Picture 500 passionate young adults that are hungry for a move of God not just in the nation of Brazil, but around the world. The atmosphere was electric. We had just found out that we were pregnant with Zion on the way over there and while there, he was baptized in the Holy Spirit while in my womb. It was special for many reasons. They asked me to speak and I remember before I even had a chance to think about it, I said yes. I remember being shocked as if, "Did I just say that? But wait a second. Let me think about this." At that moment, the Holy Spirit whispered to me, "this time is going to be different." And it was.

I got up there having embraced my authority and the place erupted. I remember coming off stage and in that moment, I fell to the floor in tears. I had found my roar. Hot tears streaming down my face, I heard the Holy Spirit say, "Your roar, full of fire - that impact, the importance that you carry - has been there all along. You just needed to give yourself permission to let it out." That moment marked me for eternity.

Deborah's life teaches us that true leadership starts with recognizing your own importance. Despite societal expectations, Deborah saw herself not just as a judge or prophetess, but as a queen with God-given authority. She understood the power of her words, which moved nations and inspired action.

Deborah didn't shrink back; she embraced her divine purpose, speaking with authority because she knew her words were backed by God. I could have shrunk back because of all my past experiences, but I stepped up knowing too, that my words were backed by God. Her confidence came from seeing the bigger picture and knowing her role was vital in fulfilling God's plan.

Like Deborah, you are called to think BIG and see yourself as significant. Your words have power, and your role in God's plan is essential. Embrace your authority, speak with confidence, and step into the purpose you were created for.

Occupy The Position of Faith

Deborah exemplified what it means to occupy the position of faith. She fully embraced her role with unwavering belief in God's promises, showing active, bold faith in her words and actions. When God commanded, Deborah acted confidently, trusting in God's power, not her own abilities. Her faith was the foundation of her leadership, enabling her to guide and inspire with conviction.

To occupy the position of faith like Deborah is to trust fully in God's plan and act on that trust. It's about being bold, knowing God is guiding you. Deborah's example teaches us that true faith is active, confident, and rooted in God's unshakable promises, empowering us to lead and inspire with certainty.

Living Like Deborah

In conclusion, the power of words, as exemplified by Deborah, is a profound reminder of the authority and influence that God has entrusted to those who walk in His purpose. Deborah's life shows us that the sweetness of honey—symbolizing wisdom, healing, and divine insight—flows from a heart aligned with God's Word. Just as her name carried the essence of her calling, our words, too, have the power to shape destinies, inspire action, and bring about change.

As you reflect on your own name, remember that God can make your name great (Genesis 12:2) and align it with His will, just as He did for Abraham. If your name's meaning doesn't feel like it fits, trust that God can redefine and repurpose any identity to fulfill His promises - just as He renamed Abram to Abraham. Embrace the truth that your voice carries weight and your words can be sweet as honey, full of God's wisdom and power.

Let your speech be infused with divine purpose and confidence. Like Deborah, understand that you are a queen, entrusted with a vital role in God's plan. Speak boldly, act in faith, and occupy the position of authority God has given you. You were designed to bring light and life to those around you. Embrace that your words reflect that calling, and watch as you, too, move nations with the power of your voice. Let's now step into the final step in our journey where you embrace your defining moment like Esther.

The Voice Of A Queen

♛ Your Defining Moment ♛
The Choice Is Yours

> *"For if you remain completely silent at this time, relief and deliverance will arise for the Jews from another place, but you and your father's house will perish. Yet who knows whether you have come to the kingdom for such a time as this?"*
> *Esther 4:14, NKJV.*

Before we begin, I want you to think back to a defining moment that changed everything for you. It might have happened years ago, or perhaps you're still waiting for that spark. Maybe you'll discover it right here, in these pages. Wherever you are - whether you've lived that moment, are on the brink of it, or are still preparing - take a moment now. Let your mind wander to that life altering time and hold on to how it made you feel. Now, let's begin.

"Chantal, your season is upon you and you know it. We've had conversations about it, we've talked about it, but you have stood at the barrier of 'how'. You don't always see it, it's hard to see sometimes, you can write something down and I can tell you just like this: You are standing at the door and the door is opening. Don't you dare give up now from walking through that door. The Lord is saying 'meet Me on the other side.'"

I sat there with tears streaming down my face as this man of God prophesied over my life. I call it my divine intervention moment. It's often tempting to linger in a state of "preparation," telling ourselves that the timing isn't right, that we need more research, or that more clarity is required. We convince ourselves that we're gearing up for something great, but the truth is, we remain in this preparatory phase far longer than necessary. Why? Because preparation feels safe. It's a comfortable place where the possibility of failure remains theoretical, not yet real. In this space, the fear of criticism, rejection, or irrelevance is kept at bay.

For me, the temptation to stay silent and remain in the comfort of obscurity was strong. I grappled with questions that many authors face: *What if no one reads my book? What if it's not good enough? What if my words don't resonate with anyone?* These fears stem from a desire for validation and a deep-seated dread of rejection.

It's natural to want our work to be appreciated, to be meaningful, and to make a difference. But the reality is that every meaningful endeavor carries the risk of failure. This process forced me to face my fears and conquer them. Every great work ever created began in a moment of uncertainty, where the creator had to choose between the safety of anonymity and the risk of stepping into the light.

Take Another Moment: As you read these lines, picture yourself in that same place of "what if."

What if you took that bold step? What if you spoke those words or wrote that book? Some of you may already know your answers. Others might be on the verge. And some might feel you're still preparing, silently gathering courage to step into your purpose as a Queen. Wherever you stand, allow yourself to feel both the fear and the possibility.

In the midst of this internal struggle, I found myself reflecting on Esther's story. Her fear of approaching the king mirrored my own fear of stepping forward with my writing. Just as Esther feared for her life, I feared for the life of my book—the life it might or might not have in the world.

Yet, like Esther, I came to understand that the cost of staying silent was far greater than the fear of stepping forward. The thought that haunted me most wasn't the possibility of failure, but the possibility that someone, somewhere, might miss out on a life-changing moment because I chose not to write. I knew the impact that God wanted to have through this book and realized that not writing it would be far more costly.

A Journey of Courage and Divine Purpose

Esther's story is a profound example of courage, faith, and the unfolding of divine plans. Esther, a young Jewish woman living in Persia, rises from obscurity to become the queen of a vast empire. Her story is one of destiny, where her choices—whether to act or remain silent—determine the fate of her people. I often find myself drawn back to Esther's account, as it resonates deeply with my own experience of stepping out of obscurity and speaking up when it matters most.

Esther's journey begins when she is selected as queen by King Ahasuerus (Xerxes) after Queen Vashti is deposed. Unbeknownst to the king, Esther is Jewish, a descendant of exiles from Jerusalem. Her cousin and guardian, Mordecai, uncovers a plot by Haman, a powerful official, to destroy the Jewish people within the kingdom. Mordecai urges Esther to approach the king and plead for the lives of her people.

However, this is no small request. The law of the land dictates that anyone who approaches the king without being summoned could be executed unless the king extends his golden scepter (Esther 4:11, NKJV). Esther hesitates, fully aware of the life-threatening risk. But Mordecai's words challenge her to see the greater purpose in her position:

"For if you remain completely silent at this time, relief and deliverance will arise for the Jews from another place, but you and your father's house will perish. Yet who knows whether you have come to the kingdom for such a time as this?" (Esther 4:14, NKJV)

This moment is the turning point in Esther's story. She decides to risk everything, declaring, "I will go to the king, which is against the law; and if I perish, I perish!" (Esther 4:16, NKJV). Her bravery and willingness to speak out save her people from destruction.

The Power of Speaking Out

Esther's story vividly illustrates the critical importance of stepping out of obscurity and having the courage to speak up when it matters most. Her initial fear of approaching the king is something we can all relate to—a fear of the unknown, of being rejected, and of potential failure. These fears often keep us silent.

Yet Esther's story shows us that the greater tragedy is not in failing but in never trying. Faced with the choice between risking her life by speaking up or ensuring the destruction of her people by staying silent, Esther chose courage, understanding that inaction would guarantee disaster.

This principle extends far beyond ancient Persia. Whether we are standing up against injustice, sharing an unpopular opinion, or pursuing a dream that others might not understand and that seems impossible, the true failure lies in never making the attempt. By staying silent, we let opportunities slip away, and we allow injustices or unmet needs to go unchallenged.

The real failure isn't in trying and falling short; it's in doing nothing at all. Esther's story is a powerful reminder that while the unknown is intimidating, the consequences of silence can be far more devastating. It is through taking action - despite our fears - that we effect change, inspire others, and fulfill our purpose.

Reflect on your own voice. Has there been a time in your life when you felt called to speak or act, yet fear held you back? Maybe that time is now. Think about what's at stake if you remain silent. How different might the outcome be if you choose, instead, to find your voice? Your defining moment might be waiting for you to speak up.

Courageous Authorship

Just as Esther faced a pivotal moment where her decision would determine the fate of an entire people, I too encountered a defining moment in my journey as an author—a moment that required courage, faith, and the willingness to step out from the shadows. Writing this book wasn't simply an act of creation; it was a confrontation with my own fears, insecurities, and the persistent question: *What if I fail?*

Esther's decision to speak up wasn't just about her; it was about the countless lives that depended on her courage. Similarly, I realized that my words—whether they reached many or just a few—had the potential to impact lives in ways I could never predict. What if there was someone out there waiting for the inspiration, guidance, or encouragement that only my book could provide? What if the words God placed inside of me were exactly what someone needed to hear to overcome their own challenges, to step into their own purpose?

In choosing to write, I chose to believe that my words mattered. I chose to believe that my voice could make a difference, even if I couldn't yet see the full extent of that impact. It was a leap of faith, much like Esther's decision to approach the king, but it was a leap I knew I had to take.

The Power of Your Voice

This experience has taught me that each of us possesses a unique voice and a message that the world needs to hear. Just as Esther's voice saved her people, our voices can unlock potential, heal wounds, and inspire change in others. But this can only happen if we're willing to speak up, to step out of our comfort zones, and to share the message God has placed inside of us with the world.

Who is waiting for your words? Who might be struggling in silence, longing for the very encouragement or wisdom that only you can provide? Your words hold power—the power to bring life, to uplift, and to transform. But they can only do so if you choose to use them.

Remember, the fear of failure should never overshadow the potential impact of your words. The world is waiting for your story, your insights, your perspective. Don't let fear keep you in the shadows. Step forward, speak up, and let your voice be heard.

Just as Esther found her courage when the stakes were high, you too can rise above your fears and share your message with the world. The journey may be challenging, and the risks may feel overwhelming, but the reward—the knowledge that you allowed God to use you to make a difference in someone's life that changed the trajectory of their future —is worth every step.

The Call to Action: Who Needs Your Words?

Esther's story compels us to reflect deeply on the immense power of our words and actions. It transcends time, urging us to recognize the unique influence we each possess. As Esther was positioned at a critical moment in history to speak up for her people, so too are we positioned in our own lives to use our voices to bring about change, healing, and inspiration. The question we must ask ourselves is this: Who is waiting for our words? Who is out there, struggling in silence, desperate for the very encouragement, wisdom, or truth that only we can offer?

The Bible reminds us that "the power of life and death is in the tongue" (Proverbs 18:21, NKJV). Our words can build up or tear down, heal or harm, inspire or discourage. They carry the potential to breathe life into situations, uplift the weary, and spark hope in hearts that have grown cold. But this only happens if we choose to speak out. Silence in the face of hardship or injustice can be just as damaging as negative words. By holding back, we may deny someone the lifeline they desperately need.

Choosing to remain silent doesn't just affect us—it affects everyone who could benefit from what we have to say. When we hide our light under a basket (Matthew 5:15, NKJV), we deny the world the brightness and clarity it so desperately needs. The light we carry—the insights, the experiences, the truths we hold—are not just for us. They are meant to be shared, to illuminate the paths of others. Like Esther, we must recognize there is a time to be silent and a time to speak, and when that time comes, we must not let fear hold us back.

In today's world, where confusion, fear, and uncertainty abound, your voice can be a beacon of hope, truth, and transformation. The ripple effect of your words can touch lives, communities, and future generations. But that impact can only happen if you choose to step out of your comfort zone and speak up. Whether it's offering a word of encouragement to a friend, sharing your story with a wider audience, or standing up against injustice, your voice matters.

As you stand at the threshold of your next chapter, think about who needs your words today. Is it someone in your family? A friend? A complete stranger who stumbles upon your story? Perhaps it's the person you'll become as you find the courage to speak.

Some of you have already experienced that defining moment. Others are finding it right now in these pages. And some of you are ready - right on the edge - preparing to walk boldly into your purpose as a Queen. Wherever you are, don't hold back. Your voice could be the spark that lights another person's path.

Conclusion

Esther's story transcends its historical context to offer us a profound and enduring lesson on the impact of our words and actions. It reminds us that even in the face of great fear and uncertainty, our choices have the power to shape destinies - ours and others'. Esther's courage to step out of her comfort zone and into her divine purpose not only saved a nation but also left a timeless example of what it means to act with conviction, even when the odds seem impossible.

Her journey from obscurity to influence shows us that our voices, no matter how small or insignificant they may seem, have the power to bring about profound change. Like Esther, we may be called to make decisions that require us to confront our deepest fears—fear of rejection, fear of failure, fear of the unknown. But it's in these moments of decision that our true character is revealed, and our greatest impact is made.

Imagine the lives that you could touch, the injustices that you could challenge, and the dreams that you could awaken by stepping up and speaking out. Each of us has a unique message, a story, or a piece of wisdom that someone out there desperately needs to hear. By allowing fear or doubt to silence us, we diminish our own potential and rob others of the hope, encouragement, or guidance that our words could provide.

When we choose to remain silent, we allow the forces of fear and doubt to set the course of our lives, missing out on extraordinary possibilities that lie beyond our comfort zones. But when we step out in faith, embracing the unknown and trusting in the purpose behind our words, we unlock a world of limitless possibilities.

Who is waiting for your words today?

The world is full of people seeking inspiration, guidance, and hope - don't keep them waiting. Your words carry the power to transform, to heal, and to empower. Don't let the fear or double hold you back. Step into the light, speak your truth, and watch as you change the world for the better - simply because you had the courage to let your voice be heard.

You've come this far - this is your defining moment. Embrace it. Seize it. Let your voice echo through the pages of your own life story. And if you feel that door swinging open before you, don't you dare turn away. Walk through it with courage, with faith, and with the unshakable conviction that you have indeed come to the kingdom for such a time as this.

The Voice Of A Queen

♛ The Final Mandate ♛

As you stand at the threshold of a new chapter, remember this: your life is far from ordinary—it is woven with the extraordinary fabric of the Kingdom of God. You are not just another face in the crowd; you are set apart, destined for a life that reflects the majesty, righteousness, and glory of the King you serve.

This is not just a calling; it is a divine mandate on your life. Your words, therefore, are not mere expressions—they are royal decrees that carry the full weight and authority of Heaven itself. When you align your speech with divine truth, you do more than communicate; you join in the sacred act of creation, shaping a reality that mirrors the power, purpose, and authority of your King.

Every time you speak His Word, you are wielding a weapon crafted in the fires of divine wisdom—a weapon that no force can resist or ignore. This is the true essence of spiritual warfare: knowing that your words, when spoken in alignment with God's will, become an unstoppable force. They do not simply resonate in the air; they pierce the very fabric of the natural world, causing Heaven to touch earth.

Your declarations, infused with faith, are not just hopeful wishes; they are the substance of miracles. Faith is the spark that transforms your words from mere utterances into powerful forces that can shape reality. Without faith, your words may fade, but with it, they become the very embodiment of God's promises, capable of bringing the impossible into existence.

True transformation occurs when you speak not only to the surface but to the very root of a matter. The power of your words goes beyond addressing symptoms; you have been given the authority to reach into the depths, to speak directly to the core. You are equipped to uproot what is destructive and plant seeds of life.

Your discernment, sharpened by divine wisdom, allows you to cut through the noise and address the heart of every situation, bringing about true and lasting change. But remember, true power is also found in restraint. There is a profound strength in knowing when to hold your peace, in embracing the divine silence that allows God's full purpose to unfold.

As a woman, your voice carries a unique and powerful anointing. You are not just another voice in the Kingdom; you are a vital force within it. Your words are not just the expressions of your thoughts and emotions; they are instruments of God's will, carrying the power to bring life, healing, and transformation.

When your words flow from a place of inner purity and strength, they become a healing balm, a source of life that nourishes and uplifts all who hear them. Never underestimate the power that resides within you. The greatest failure is not in speaking and risking failure; it is in choosing silence when your words could have sparked change, birthed hope, or altered the course of destiny.

Now is the time to step into your God-given authority with boldness and confidence. Speak knowing that your words are not just your own—they are the echoes of the divine, the very voice of the King resounding through you.

Let your life be a radiant testimony of the Kingdom, a living reflection of God's glory on earth. Let your words create, transform, and heal, bringing a touch of Heaven to every situation you encounter. And let your faith be the driving force that turns every declaration into a tangible reality. You are not just a woman; you are royalty, chosen and anointed for such a time as this. With your words, you will shape nations, change lives, and fulfill the divine purpose for which you were created.

Step forward, speak boldly, and let the world be forever transformed by the power of your words, for you are a queen, and the world awaits the impact of your voice.

The choice is yours.

Do you accept your divine mandate as a Queen?

The King is waiting!

The Voice Of A Queen

👑 ACKNOWLEDGEMENTS 👑

First and foremost, to my Lord and King, my God, my Source—every word in this book exists because of You. You are the Author of my life, the One who knows the end from the beginning, the One who gave me this message, and the One who speaks through me. Thank You for entrusting me with this assignment, for revealing deep truths, and for making this moment possible. May this book glorify You and awaken the queens You have called to rise.

To my love, Christian—my warrior, my covering, my greatest encourager. Your wisdom, your revelations, and your unwavering belief in me have carried me through this process. Thank you for the late-night conversations, the deep insights, and for always pushing me to step fully into my God-given authority. I love you beyond words.

To my children, Zion and Zara—you are my greatest joy and my reason for living out the truth of these pages. Zion, your strength and resilience inspire me daily, and to Zara, your presence reminds me of the power of a mother's voice. May you both grow up knowing the weight and authority your words carry.

To my core—my inner circle—you know who you are. The ones who prayed for me and with me, encouraged me, reminded me of the assignment when I wanted to retreat. Your words strengthened me. Your belief in this book fueled my fire. I am eternally grateful for each of you.

To my main editors and proofreaders—Christian, Jasma & Janelle (Mum) - your sharp eyes, thoughtful feedback, and dedication made this book the powerful piece it is today. Thank you for your patience, your excellence, and your heart for this message.

To my Pre-Launch Team—the ones who got to read these words before the world did. Your excitement, your testimonies, and your willingness to champion this book during the writing process meant more than you know. Thank you for standing with me and for seeing the vision before it was fully formed.

To my future readers—to the queens, the women of God, the ones searching for their voice and reclaiming their authority—I wrote this for you. May these words remind you of who you are, embolden you to speak life, and empower you to unleash the power of purposeful words. You are not just reading this book; you are stepping into a royal decree over your life.

With all my love and gratitude,

Chantal Santiago

ABOUT THE AUTHOR

Chantal Santiago is an inspiring, bold Kingdom communicator and author of *The Voice Of A Queen: Unleashing The Power Of Purposeful Words*. As a devoted wife, mother, and co-founder of Born To Rule Global alongside her husband, Christian, she empowers faith-driven women to live boldly and embrace their God-given authority.

As a Kingdom Breakthrough & Transformation Specialist, Chantal is dedicated to helping women unlock their fullest potential by drawing them into a vibrant, experiential understanding of the Kingdom of God—a realm where divine power, anointing, and freedom are as real on earth as they are in heaven.

With a passionate, heart-stirring speaking style, Chantal offers a clear, practical roadmap for those who feel stuck, broken, or unsure of their next steps. She shares her own raw journey of faith—its struggles, victories, and hard-won lessons—to demonstrate that true transformation begins at the feet of Jesus.

By utilizing faith, boldness, and an assured identity, she reveals how every believer can activate the heavenly power and anointing here on earth, experiencing the same divine truth and restoration that defines the Kingdom of Heaven.

Driven by compassion, authenticity, and unshakable faith, Chantal challenges women to step into their destiny as living testimonies of God's love and power. Her deepest desire is to see a generation of faith-filled women rise up, conquer obstacles, and change the world—one courageous, Kingdom-driven step at a time.

The Voice Of A Queen

www.ingramcontent.com/pod-product-compliance
Ingram Content Group UK Ltd.
Pitfield, Milton Keynes, MK11 3LW, UK
UKHW050817090425
5388UKWH00012B/139/J